HIKING SOUTHERN ARIZONA

by

Don R. Kiefer

GOLDEN WEST ☼ PUBLISHERS

Cover photo: "Hiking the Old Baldy Trail" by Christine M. Hamel

Library of Congress Cataloging-in-Publication Data

Kiefer, Don R.
Hiking Southern Arizona / by Don R. Kiefer
   p.   cm.
Includes index.
1. Hiking—Arizona—Guidebooks.   2. Arizona—Guidebooks.
   I. Title.
GV199.42.A7K56 1995   95-44586
796.5' 1'09791—dc20   CIP

Printed in the United States of America

1st Printing © 1995

ISBN #1-885590-10-5

Golden West Publishers, Inc.
4113 N. Longview Ave.
Phoenix, AZ 85014, USA
(602) 265-4392

Dedication

To my son, Monte, and his wife, Julie, who have started their young lives together in the mountains of North Carolina.

May they enjoy as much happiness in their lives together as I have in writing this book.

Acknowledgements

It is my belief that every author has the help of someone else in creating a book. This book was no exception.

A lot of my help was received from the following:

The many agencies listed in this book under, "Where to obtain more information for trails in this book".

MARICOPA CIVIL DEFENSE & EMERGENCY SERVICES with their excellent survival tips.

MESA TRIBUNE for having given me a chance to prove my writing skills.

ROBYN WASSERMAN, Vail, Arizona, who was asked for so much in drawing all my maps, never complaining when finding out that, yes, there's more!

Last but not least, EVELYN LONG, Gilbert, Arizona. She has been both my left and right hands since 1986. My career would not be where it is today without her kindness when preparing my work for the publisher.

I fully realize that this book was a team effort.

Thanks to everyone!

Don Kiefer

Southern Trails

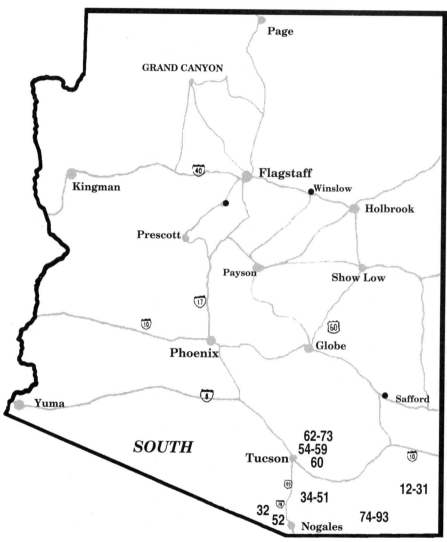

Page

GRAND CANYON

Kingman

I-40 Flagstaff Winslow

Holbrook

Prescott

Payson Show Low

I-17

I-10 US-60

Phoenix Globe

Yuma I-8 Safford

SOUTH

62-73
54-59
Tucson 60

I-10

12-31

US-89

34-51

32 I-19
52 74-93
Nogales

Numbers on map refer to page numbers in book

Southern Arizona Hiking Trails
TABLE OF CONTENTS

HIKING SOUTHERN ARIZONA TRAILS

(Continued on next page)

Hiking Tips from the Author

• Be sure that you have the appropriate topographic maps, and bring this book along too! You may find some of the information included here of lifesaving value!

• If possible, include a cellular phone in your camping equipment—they have proven invaluable on many occasions.

• Use the "buddy system" whenever possible. A friend in need is a friend indeed!

• Always leave information with someone as to where you are going and how long you expect to be gone and remember . . . that information is of no value to anyone if you do not follow your original plans.

• Be sure to check that you have the Day Pack and Backpack items listed on page 98 as your hike requires.

• Check the weather forecast before you leave on your hike.

Introduction

ARIZONA! What would it be like to hike it all? We will never know; one's life span was not designed to allow enough time for any one man or woman to accomplish this.

This book which is part of a new hiking Arizona series *(Hiking Northern Arizona, Hiking Central Arizona,* and *Hiking Southern Arizona)* will provide you with the tools, if used properly, to move you closer to having "hiked it all."

Get ready to either enjoy, or tolerate, the lowland deserts. They make up an area soft with fresh scents, the gentle buzzing of the bees and the silent wanderings of the butterflies. The desert's other side is the extreme heat, many venomous creatures, and storms more vicious than you can imagine.

Also prepare yourself for high altitudes and, yes, even true tundra conditions right here in Arizona. There are areas so quiet you will think you have lost your hearing, with visibility beyond what you thought you could ever see, and so remote you will wonder if there is a way home. Of course, the other extreme exists here as well: snowstorms any day of the year, so much static electricity in the air that your clothes will crack with each step, making it sound as if you are walking on potato chips, 50 m.p.h. winds—Mother Nature on a bad day—and creatures that outweigh you by three and four times that hopefully just watch you go by.

Always thoroughly acquaint yourself with the trail you wish to hike, obtain and study the maps required and, most of all, know and obey your own limitations.

Please be aware that due to funding cutbacks many of Arizona's trails are not in the condition we would like to find them. Currently, volunteers are needed to assist trail maintenance crews. If you would like to aid in this work, please contact the trail managing agency of your choice.

Don Kiefer

As you read this book, you may wonder why some of the other major trails in Arizona are not included. The reason is that they are included in my two previous books, *Hiking Arizona* and *Hiking Arizona II.*—D.K.

HOW TO READ THE STAT PAGES

ATTRACTION: Self-explanatory

REQUIREMENTS: These are things that cannot be stressed enough. Study the contents of your day packs and backpacks.

LOCATION: This is the general area; your maps will do the rest.

DIFFICULTY: This will vary with different people; if anything, some are overrated.

ELEVATIONS: Most elevations are approximate, but close.

LENGTH: Most mileages are approximate, but close.

MAPS REQUIRED: Although I have listed the proper topo maps, you must be aware that all trails are not on these maps, but contour lines and altitudes are. You must use the proper Forest Service maps for the corresponding areas. These have not only the trails but roads as well. You can find both maps at good map stores or the proper ranger stations.

PERMIT: Although most districts do not require a permit for you to hike, permits are needed for large groups or special activities. You must check with the appropriate agencies to be sure.

BIKES: Never permitted in a wilderness area or where posted. I have indicated "No" on a lot of trails simply because bike riding would be very impractical.

EQUESTRIAN: Horses are allowed on most trails, but you must study your altitudes and grades and be sure your horse is able to safely negotiate them.

WATER: Even though I have said "Yes" on many trails, I have still recommended that you bring your own water. It's always best to drink water you are used to.

INFORMATION: These are usually points to be stressed or helpful tips.

FIREARMS: When I say "Yes" on firearms, it does not mean you need one, rather that you may carry one if you choose. I have never had any use for one in all my hiking experience, and certainly would not like the extra weight.

PETS: Although pets are not strictly forbidden on most Forest Service trails, you still have many responsibilities. **Your pet is to be contained.** Your pet is to be very obedient or on a leash. Your pet must not be permitted to chase wildlife or to scare others on foot or horseback.

TRAIL INFORMATION: This will contain directions to trailheads along with the trail information itself.

All of the above information is to be thoroughly studied before ever setting foot on a trail if you are to have a good hike.

Reading Trail Signs

"How elementary!" you may say. When you come upon a sign that reads, "Peach Springs - 2.5 miles," how hard can it be to understand? Let's consider this, however. You get caught in a snowstorm and it dumps about four inches of snow and the terrain becomes level (it happened to me). Except for distance, the above trail sign is of no more value; it is obvious that you need to look for other trail signs besides a post and a board.

1. Chevrons

Chevrons are metal tabs about three inches square, that are tacked to trees along the trail about six to eight feet above the ground. The ones I have seen have been white, orange or red. You must be careful not to lose sight of the one you just passed before the next one comes into view. Some trees will have two chevrons indicating either that another trail connects the trail you are on, or that there is a very sharp turn in your trail. Take a minute to study the area well when two chevrons are encountered. Chevrons are found mostly in high altitudes.

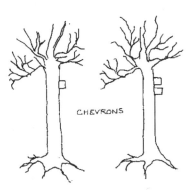

CHEVRONS

2. Tree Notches

These notches are carved into trees at about the five to six-foot level. Most are about 3/4 inch deep and have rounded edges because of the tree's ability to eventually heal over the notch. They are a little harder to spot as they take on the same color as the tree. Notches sometimes are found in the lower altitudes as well. They are interpreted exactly the same as chevrons.

TREE
NOTCHES

3. Cairns

Cairns are very expertly arranged stacks of rocks along the trail, graduating from a large base to almost a point. I have seen them from ten inches high to four feet high, and they simply guide your way. These are found on areas of trails that are just rock surfaces, where a path will never be worn and there are no trees for chevrons or notches. Believe me, it's a very hit-and-miss situation getting through areas like this without a scattering of rock cairns.

As you can see, trail signs come in many forms and it is a good idea to train yourself to spot them, even though you may not be having any problems finding your way.

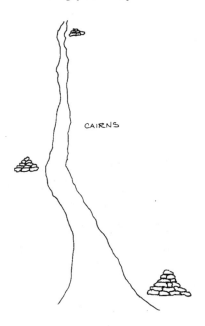

CAIRNS

Hiking
Southern
Arizona

JHUS-HORSE SADDLE TRAIL #252

ATTRACTION: Very remote and uncrowded, old mining area.

REQUIREMENTS: Food, water, sturdy boots, maps; car okay to Pinery-Horsefall trailhead; 3/4 hour hiking time one way.

LOCATION: Douglas Ranger District - Chiricahua Mountains.

DIFFICULTY: Difficult

ELEVATIONS: 5960' - 7040' (with Pinery-Horsefall Trail #336).

LENGTH: 1 mile one way.

MAPS REQUIRED: U.S.G.S. 7.5 min. topographic for Rustler Park.

PERMIT: No

BIKES: No

EQUESTRIAN: Yes

WATER: No - bring your own.

INFORMATION: Best access to this trail is from the Pinery-Horsefall Trail #336. Getting to actual trailhead of Jhus-Horse Saddle Trail requires 4-wheel drive only!

FIREARMS: Yes

PETS ON LEASH: Yes

TRAIL INFORMATION

Travel east on I-10 from Tucson for about 80 miles and turn right on AZ 186. In about 23 miles, make a left turn on AZ 181 and travel 4 miles to Forest Road #42. Turn right and take Forest Road #42 to the trailhead of Pinery-Horsefall Trail #336, about 6 miles (recommended access).

The trailhead for Jhus-Horse Saddle Trail is at the end of Forest Road #341 from East Whitetail Canyon (4-wheel drive only). See map.

Pinery-Horsefall Trail #336 leaves Pinery Canyon as it slowly climbs over a ridgetop into the very lush green Horsefall Canyon. Your travel will be along this canyon as you climb to Jhus-Horse Saddle and the junction of Jhus-Horse Saddle Trail #252. About 200 feet north of this junction the Shaw Peak Trail #251 crosses from the northwest to the southeast.

The Jhus-Horse Saddle Trail slowly descends through some small drainages to an old mining area at the end of Forest Road #341 (4-wheel drive). Return the same way.

JHUS-HORSE SADDLE
TRAIL #252

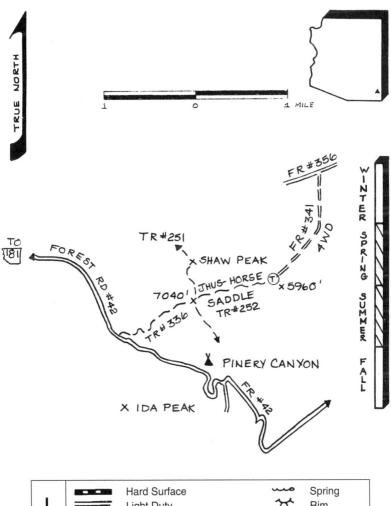

LEGEND

▬▬ ▬ ▬	Hard Surface	⌐⌐o Spring
═══	Light Duty	⋎⋎⋎ Rim
═ ═ ═ ═	Unimproved	⌐ Corral
‑ ‑ ‑ ‑	Trail	× Peak
+++++	Railroad	Ⓣ Trailhead
■ ■	Buildings	P. Parking
O	Water Tank	ᗫ Water
⚑	Campsite	⌒ River
×5270	Elevation Check	⌒...⌒. Drainage

MORMON CANYON TRAIL #352

ATTRACTION: High country hiking through riparian areas and many breathtaking views.

REQUIREMENTS: Food, water, sturdy boots, proper maps; car okay to trailhead; 2.5 hours hiking time one way.

LOCATION: Douglas Ranger District - Chiricahua Mountains.

DIFFICULTY: Difficult

ELEVATIONS: 6180' - 9240'   **LENGTH:** 3.4 miles one way.

MAPS REQUIRED: U.S.G.S. 7.5 min. topographic for Chiricahua Peak-Rustler Park.

PERMIT: No   **BIKES:** No

EQUESTRIAN: Yes   **WATER:** No - bring your own.

INFORMATION: Altitudes above pretty well cover Saulsbury Trail #263, Mormon Ridge Trail #269 and Mormon Canyon Trail #352. Study for loop hike for all three trails.

FIREARMS: Yes   **PETS ON LEASH:** Yes

TRAIL INFORMATION

Travel east on I-10 out of Tucson just over 70 miles to U.S. 191. Make a right turn and continue just over 20 miles to AZ 181. Take 181 east for about 12 miles to the Turkey Creek turnoff (Forest Road #41). Follow Forest Road #41 to Forest Road #632 (8 miles). Saulsbury Trail trailhead is located on Forest Road #632.

The trailheads for Mormon Canyon Trail #352 and Mormon Ridge Trail #269 are located on Forest Road #41 at Sycamore Campground.

Mormon Canyon Trail and Mormon Ridge Trail are located south of Saulsbury Trail #263. Mormon Ridge Trail should be used as a descending hike when using it as a loop, as trail is very steep.

Just before Mormon Canyon, these trails cross each other with Mormon Ridge Trail traveling north to Cima Park and Mormon Canyon Trail going south to Chiricahua Saddle, both located on Crest Trail #270.

Return the same way or build a loop hike via Crest Trail #270 and trails listed under INFORMATION.

MORMON CANYON
TRAIL #352

TRUE NORTH

1 0 1 MILE

W I N T E R   S P R I N G   S U M M E R   F A L L

W. TURKEY CREEK

FLYS PEAK
×

TO
181

FR #41

6180'×

T

TR #269

TR #352

MORMON CYN   ×9240'

CHIRICAHUA ×9796'
PEAK

×9357'
MONTE VISTA PEAK

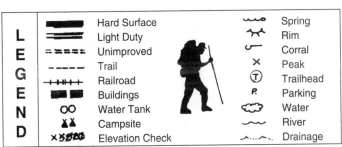

L E G E N D		
▬▬▬ Hard Surface	~~o	Spring
═══ Light Duty	⌣⌣	Rim
═ ═ ═ Unimproved	⌣	Corral
‑ ‑ ‑ ‑ Trail	×	Peak
‑+‑+‑+ Railroad	Ⓣ	Trailhead
▬ ▬ Buildings	P.	Parking
oo Water Tank	☁	Water
⚑⚑ Campsite	~~	River
×5920 Elevation Check	~...~.	Drainage

MORMON RIDGE TRAIL #269

ATTRACTION: High country hiking through riparian areas and many breathtaking views.

REQUIREMENTS: Food, water, sturdy boots, proper maps; car okay to trailhead; 3 hours hiking time one way.

LOCATION: Douglas Ranger District - Chiricahua Mountains.

DIFFICULTY: Difficult

ELEVATIONS: 6180 - 9240'

LENGTH: 4.5 miles one way.

MAPS REQUIRED: U.S.G.S. 7.5 min. topographic for Chiricahua Peak-Rustler Park.

PERMIT: No   **BIKES:** No

EQUESTRIAN: Yes   **WATER:** No - bring your own.

INFORMATION: Altitudes above pretty well cover Saulsbury Trail #263, Mormon Ridge Trail #269 and Mormon Canyon Trail #352. Study for loop hike for all three trails.

FIREARMS: Yes   **PETS ON LEASH:** Yes

TRAIL INFORMATION

Travel east on I-10 out of Tucson just over 70 miles to U.S. 191. Make a right turn and continue for just over 20 miles to AZ 181. Take 181 east for about 12 miles to the Turkey Creek turnoff (Forest Road #41). Follow Forest Road #41 to Forest Road #632 (8 miles). Saulsbury Trail trailhead is located on Forest Road #632.

The Mormon Ridge Trail #269 and Mormon Canyon Trail #352 trailheads are both located on Forest Road #41 at Sycamore Campground. Mormon Ridge Trail and Mormon Canyon Trail are located south of Saulsbury Trail #263.

Mormon Ridge Trail should be used as a descending hike when using it as a loop, as trail is very steep. This trail can be very hot in summer as it is on a southern slope. Just before Mormon Canyon, these trails cross each other with Mormon Ridge Trail traveling north to Cima Park and Mormon Canyon Trail going south to Chiricahua Saddle, both located on Crest Trail #270.

Return same way or build a loop hike via Crest Trail #270 and trails listed under INFORMATION.

MORMON RIDGE TRAIL #269

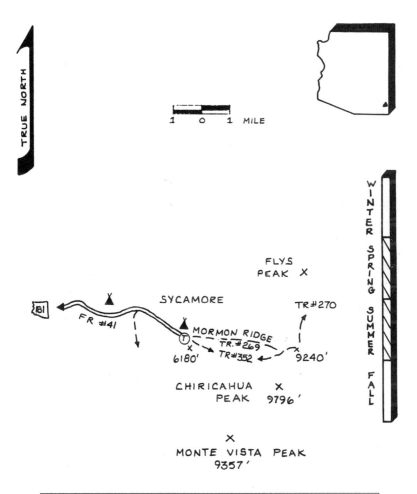

TRUE NORTH

1 0 1 MILE

WINTER SPRING SUMMER FALL

FLYS PEAK ✕

SYCAMORE

TR#270

FR #41

MORMON RIDGE
TR.#269
TR#352
6180'
9240'

CHIRICAHUA ✕
PEAK 9796'

✕
MONTE VISTA PEAK
9357'

L E G E N D				
▅▬▅	Hard Surface		∿o	Spring
═══	Light Duty		⤙	Rim
≕≕≕	Unimproved		⌐	Corral
-----	Trail		×	Peak
++++	Railroad		Ⓣ	Trailhead
■ ■	Buildings		P.	Parking
o	Water Tank		☁	Water
⚑	Campsite		∼	River
×5270	Elevation Check		∼...∼.	Drainage

MORSE CANYON TRAIL #43

ATTRACTION: Monte Vista Peak and Pole Bridge Research Area, nice forest hike.

REQUIREMENTS: Food, water, sturdy boots, proper maps; car okay to trailhead; 4.5 hours hiking time round trip.

LOCATION: Douglas Ranger District - Chiricahua Mountains.

DIFFICULTY: Difficult

ELEVATIONS: 6200' - 8600'

LENGTH: 2.4 miles one way

MAPS REQUIRED: U.S.G.S. 7.5 min. topographic for Chiricahua Peak.

PERMIT: No

BIKES: No

EQUESTRIAN: Yes

WATER: No - bring your own.

INFORMATION: Check for round trip loop via Pole Bridge Trail #264, Turtle Mountain Trail #219 and Forest Road #41.

FIREARMS: Yes   **PETS ON LEASH:** Yes

TRAIL INFORMATION

Follow I-10 east from Tucson just over 70 miles and turn right (south) on U.S. 191. In just over 20 miles make a left turn (east) on AZ 181. In just over 11 miles will be the Turkey Creek turnoff (Forest Road #41). Take Forest Road #41 for 11 miles to the trailhead of Morse Canyon Trail #43.

This trail starts to climb from the start. Your very shaded hike starts as you make your way up the most popular trail to Monte Vista Peak. The trail will be very evident, continuing to climb as you arrive at the junction of Turtle Mountain Trail #219. A left turn here onto #219 will put you on the summit of Monte Vista Peak in .5 mile.

You can return the same way or take Turtle Mountain Trail #219 back down past Morse Canyon Trail to the junction of Pole Bridge Trail #264. Make a right turn and travel 3.8 miles to its trailhead. From here it's only a short 1.5 miles to your car at Morse Canyon trailhead. Consult your map.

MORSE CANYON TRAIL #43

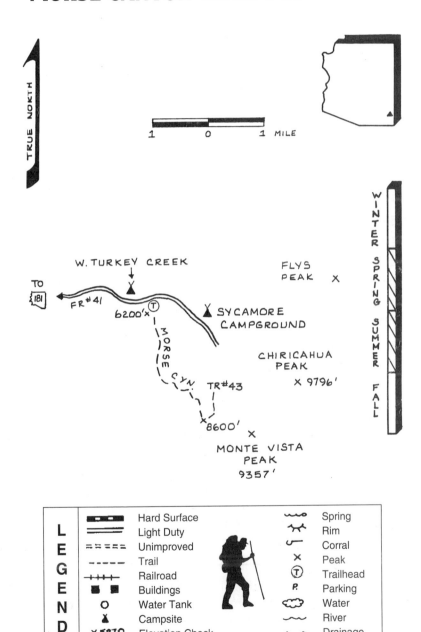

TRUE NORTH

1 0 1 MILE

WINTER SPRING SUMMER FALL

W. TURKEY CREEK

FLYS PEAK ×

TO [181]

FR#41

6200'×

(T)

MORSE CYN.

▲ SYCAMORE CAMPGROUND

CHIRICAHUA PEAK
× 9796'

TR#43

×8600' ×

MONTE VISTA PEAK
9357'

LEGEND

▬▬▬	Hard Surface	
▬▬▬	Light Duty	
≡≡≡≡≡	Unimproved	
-----	Trail	
┼┼┼┼┼	Railroad	
■ ■	Buildings	
O	Water Tank	
▲	Campsite	
×5270	Elevation Check	

〰o	Spring
⤳	Rim
⌒	Corral
×	Peak
(T)	Trailhead
P.	Parking
☁	Water
〜	River
〜…〜	Drainage

PINERY-HORSEFALL TRAIL #336

ATTRACTION: Very remote, uncrowded, nice views as you travel over the ridge.

REQUIREMENTS: Food, water, sturdy boots, proper maps; car okay to trailhead; 2 hours hiking time one way.

LOCATION: Douglas Ranger District - Chiricahua Mountains.

DIFFICULTY: Difficult

ELEVATIONS: 5960' - 7040' (with Jhus-Horse Saddle Trail #252).

LENGTH: 2.7 miles one way.

MAPS REQUIRED: U.S.G.S. 7.5 min. topographic for Rustler Park.

PERMIT: No

BIKES: Not recommended.

EQUESTRIAN: Yes

WATER: No - bring your own.

INFORMATION: This trail is also the best access to Jhus-Horse Saddle Trail #252; these trails work well together.

FIREARMS: Yes

PETS ON LEASH: Yes

TRAIL INFORMATION

Travel east on I-10 from Tucson about 80 miles and turn right on AZ 186. In about 23 miles, you will make a left turn on AZ 181 and travel 4 miles to Forest Road #42. Turn right and take Forest Road #42 6 miles to the trailhead of Pinery-Horsefall Trail #336.

Pinery-Horsefall Trail leaves Pinery Canyon as it slowly climbs into the very lush green Horsefall Canyon. Your travel will be along this canyon as you climb to Jhus-Horse Saddle and the junction of Jhus-Horse Saddle Trail #252.

About 200 feet north of this junction, the Shaw Peak Trail #251 crosses from the northwest to the southeast.

The Jhus-Horse Saddle Trail slowly descends through some small drainages to an old mining area at the end of Forest Road #341 (4-wheel drive). Return the same way.

PINERY-HORSEFALL
TRAIL #336

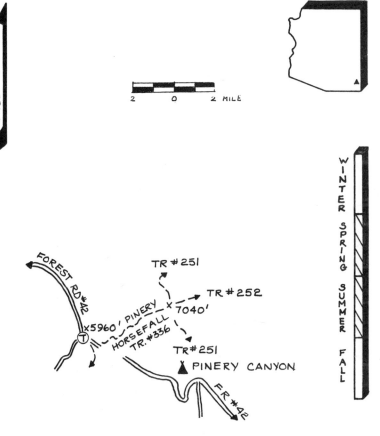

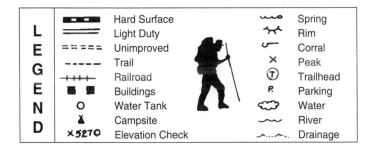

POLE BRIDGE TRAIL #264

ATTRACTION: Monte Vista Peak and Pole Bridge Research Area, nice forest hike.

REQUIREMENTS: Food, water, sturdy boots, proper maps; car okay to trailhead; 2.5 hours hiking time one way.

LOCATION: Douglas Ranger District - Chiricahua Mountains.

DIFFICULTY: Difficult

ELEVATIONS: 6200' - 8600'

LENGTH: 3.8 miles one way.

MAPS REQUIRED: U.S.G.S. 7.5 min. topographic for Chiricahua Peak.

PERMIT: No   **BIKES:** No

EQUESTRIAN: Yes   **WATER:** No - bring your own.

INFORMATION: Check for right turn loop via Turtle Mountain Trail #219, Morse Canyon Trail #43 and Forest Road #41.

FIREARMS: Yes   **PETS ON LEASH:** Yes

TRAIL INFORMATION

Follow I-10 east from Tucson just over 70 miles and turn right (south) U.S. 191. In just over 20 miles, make a left turn (east) on AZ 181. In just over 11 miles will be the Turkey Creek turnoff (Forest Road #41). Take Forest Road #41 for 9.8 miles to the trailhead of Pole Bridge Trail #264.

As you climb this trail, it will take you through the Pole Bridge Research Natural Area. Please respect what you find.

As you start to switchback towards end of trail, watch for fantastic views of West Turkey Creek Canyon and Sulpher Springs Valley.

At trail's end, if you want to continue to Monte Vista Peak (3/4 mile), then make a left turn on Turtle Mountain Trail #219, travel past the Morse Canyon Trail #43 and continue last half mile to peak. You can make a right turn loop hike down by taking a right turn on Morse Canyon Trail #43 to its trailhead. From here it is only a short 1.5 miles to your car at Pole Bridge Trail #264 trailhead. Consult your map.

POLE BRIDGE TRAIL #264

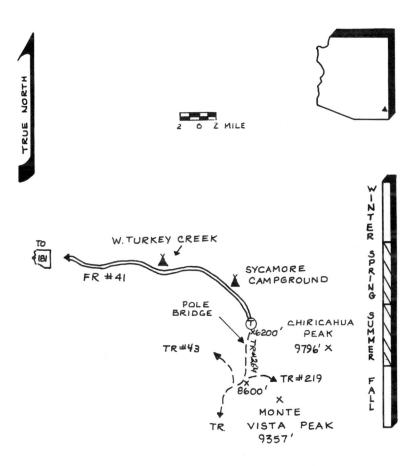

TRUE NORTH

2 0 2 MILE

W. TURKEY CREEK

SYCAMORE CAMPGROUND

FR #41

TO 181

POLE BRIDGE

×6200'

CHIRICAHUA PEAK
9796' ×

TR #43

TR #264

TR #219

×
8600'

TR.

× MONTE VISTA PEAK
9357'

WINTER SPRING SUMMER FALL

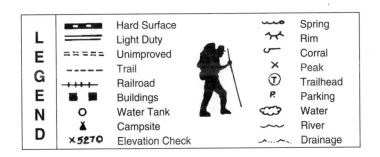

L E G E N D			
▬▬▬	Hard Surface	⌁o	Spring
▬▬▬	Light Duty	⋎⋎⋎	Rim
=====	Unimproved	⌐	Corral
-----	Trail	×	Peak
+++++	Railroad	Ⓣ	Trailhead
▪ ▪	Buildings	P.	Parking
o	Water Tank	☁	Water
▲	Campsite	⌇	River
×5270	Elevation Check	⌇...⌇.	Drainage

RATTLESNAKE TRAIL #275

ATTRACTION: Fantastic views of many high peaks.

REQUIREMENTS: Food, water, sturdy boots, proper maps; high clearance vehicle to trailhead; 5.5 hours hiking time round trip.

LOCATION: Douglas Ranger District - Chiricahua Mountains.

DIFFICULTY: Difficult

ELEVATIONS: 6500' - 8320'

LENGTH: 4 miles one way

MAPS REQUIRED: U.S.G.S. 7.5 min topographic for Rustler Park.

PERMIT: No

BIKES: No

EQUESTRIAN: Yes

WATER: Not dependable.

INFORMATION: After Forest Road #42, high-clearance vehicle recommended.

FIREARMS: Yes

PETS ON LEASH: Yes

TRAIL INFORMATION

Take I-10 east out of Tucson for about 80 miles to AZ 186. Travel south on AZ 186 to AZ 181 (about 23 miles). Travel east on AZ 181 for 4 miles to Forest Road #42 and turn south. Continue for 6 miles to Forest Road #42C, make a left turn and another left on Forest Road #357, and continue to trailhead on the right.

Trail is the remains of an old fire road. After winding back and forth across Rattlesnake Creek for a little under 1 mile, you will enter the wilderness.

In another half mile, you will start ascending to a saddle of sorts before turning east. The views are great and travel is easier now to the trail's end at the junction of Rock Creek Trail #259 and Bootlegger Trail #257.

Return the way you came.

RATTLESNAKE TRAIL #275

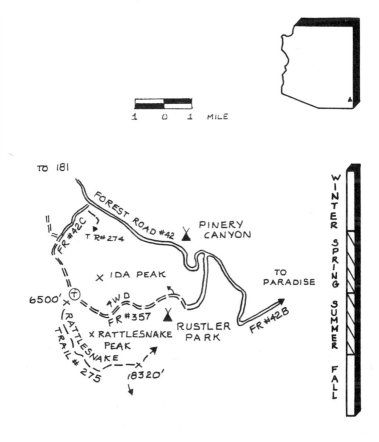

TRUE NORTH

1 0 1 MILE

WINTER SPRING SUMMER FALL

TO 181

FOREST ROAD #42

FR #42C

T R# 274

PINERY CANYON

× IDA PEAK

6500'+

4WD

FR #357

TO PARADISE

RATTLESNAKE TRAIL # 275

× RATTLESNAKE PEAK

RUSTLER PARK

FR #42B

18320'

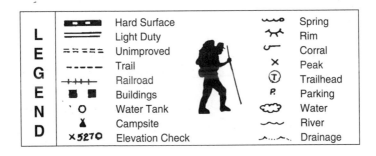

L E G E N D				
▬▬▬	Hard Surface		∽∽○	Spring
═══	Light Duty		⋏⋏	Rim
═ ═ ═ ═	Unimproved		⌒	Corral
- - - - -	Trail		×	Peak
+++++	Railroad		Ⓣ	Trailhead
▬ ▬	Buildings		P.	Parking
` ○	Water Tank		⌒⌒⌒	Water
⚑	Campsite		∽∽	River
×5270	Elevation Check		⌒…⌒.	Drainage

SAULSBURY TRAIL #263

ATTRACTION: High country hiking through riparian areas and many breathtaking views.

REQUIREMENTS: Food, water, sturdy boots, proper maps; car okay to trailhead; 3 hours hiking time one way.

LOCATION: Douglas Ranger District - Chiricahua Mountains.

DIFFICULTY: Difficult

ELEVATIONS: 6180' - 9240'

LENGTH: 4.4 miles one way.

MAPS REQUIRED: U.S.G.S. 7.5 min. topographic for Chiricahua Peak-Rustler Park.

PERMIT: No   **BIKES:** No

EQUESTRIAN: Yes   **WATER:** No - bring your own.

INFORMATION: Altitudes above pretty well cover Saulsbury Trail #263, Mormon Ridge Trail #269 and Mormon Canyon Trail #352. Study for loop hike for all three trails.

FIREARMS: Yes   **PETS ON LEASH:** Yes

TRAIL INFORMATION

Travel east on I-10 out of Tucson just over 70 miles to U.S. 191. Make a right turn and travel just over 20 miles to AZ 181. Take 181 east for about 12 miles to the Turkey Creek turnoff (Forest Road #41). Follow Forest Road #41 to Forest Road #632 (8 miles). Saulsbury Trail trailhead is located on Forest Road #632.

The Mormon Canyon Trail #352 trailhead and Mormon Ridge Trail #269 trailhead are located on Forest Road #41 at Sycamore Campground.

Saulsbury Trail leads up Saulsbury Canyon to the northeast and eventually climbs out of the canyon before climbing towards and over Little Bull Mountain. From this point it is not far to its junction with Crest Trail #270 in the vicinity of Chiricahua and Fly's Peak. You will have good views of Rock Creek and West Turkey Creek Canyons, as well as Sulpher Springs Valley.

Return the same way or build a loop hike via Crest Trail #270 and trails listed under INFORMATION.

SAULSBURY TRAIL #263

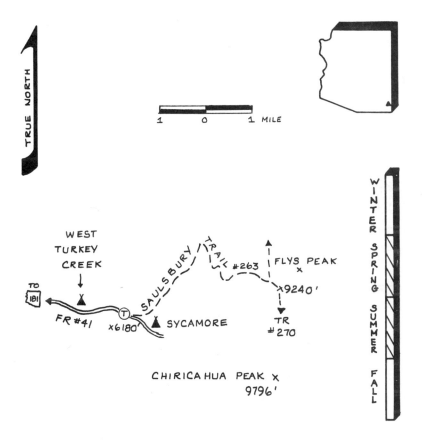

TRUE NORTH

1   0   1 MILE

WINTER SPRING SUMMER FALL

WEST
TURKEY
CREEK

SAULSBURY TRAIL   #263 FLYS PEAK x

x9240'

TO 181

FR #41   x6180' (T)   SYCAMORE   TR #270

CHIRICAHUA PEAK x
9796'

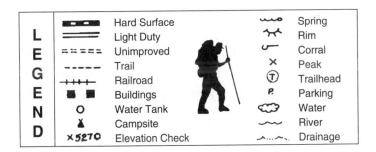

L	Hard Surface	Spring
E	Light Duty	Rim
G	Unimproved	Corral
E	Trail	× Peak
N	Railroad	(T) Trailhead
D	Buildings	P. Parking
	O Water Tank	Water
	Campsite	River
	×5270 Elevation Check	Drainage

SHAW PEAK TRAIL #251

ATTRACTION: Fantastic views, remote.

REQUIREMENTS: Food, water, sturdy boots, proper maps; 4-wheel drive vehicle to trailhead; 3.5 hours hiking time one way.

LOCATION: Douglas Ranger District - Chiricahua Mountains.

DIFFICULTY: Difficult

ELEVATIONS: 6400' - 7900'

LENGTH: 5.2 miles one way.

MAPS REQUIRED: U.S.G.S. 7.5 min. topographic for Rustler Park.

PERMIT: No

BIKES: Not recommended.

EQUESTRIAN: Yes

WATER: Not dependable.

INFORMATION: This trail can be hard to follow; not for a novice. Know how to read your maps. Truck shuttle possible.

FIREARMS: Yes   **PETS ON LEASH:** Yes

TRAIL INFORMATION

Take I-10 east from Tucson 80 miles, turn right (south) on AZ 186 and go 23 miles to AZ 181. Turn left on AZ 181, travel 4 miles to Forest Road #42 and turn right. In 6 miles turn left on Forest Road #356 (4-wheel drive) to north trailhead. You also could continue on Forest Road #42 to Onion Saddle where a left turn on Forest Road #4854 (4-wheel drive) would take you to the south trailhead.

From Onion Saddle, the trail follows a road that went to the Misfire Mine. After trail leaves this road, you will climb to the north summit of Onion Peak, to Jhus-Horse Saddle. Here Pinery-Horsefall Trail #336 turns left and Jhus-Horse Saddle Trail #252 turns right. Continue straight to Shaw Saddle and all of its fantastic views. Soon you descend to Hilltop Mine and its ruins. It is now 2.2 miles of 4-wheel-drive road along the north fork of Pinery Canyon to Forest Road #42.

Study all your options for this hike.

SHAW PEAK TRAIL #251

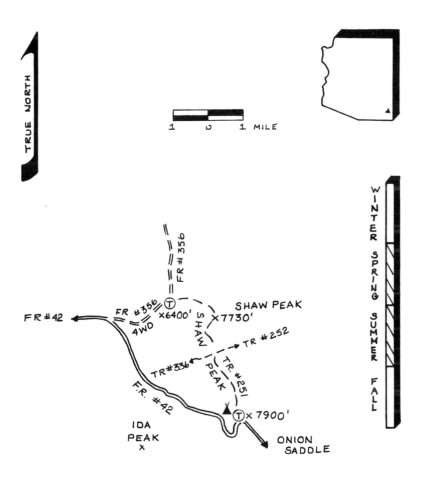

TRUE NORTH

1 0 1 MILE

WINTER SPRING SUMMER FALL

FR # 356

FR # 356
4WD

FR #42

×6400'

SHAW

SHAW PEAK
×7730'

TR #252

TR#336

TR. #251

F.R. #42

IDA
PEAK
×

×7900'

ONION
SADDLE

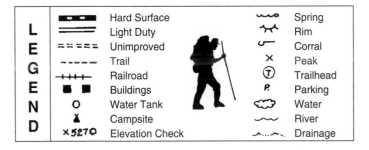

L E G E N D

Hard Surface	
Light Duty	
Unimproved	
Trail	
Railroad	
Buildings	
O Water Tank	
Campsite	
×5270 Elevation Check	

Spring	
Rim	
Corral	
× Peak	
Ⓣ Trailhead	
P. Parking	
Water	
River	
Drainage	

SOUTH FORK TRAIL #243

ATTRACTION: Access to high country along a gentle stream, fantastic views.

REQUIREMENTS: Food, water, sturdy boots, proper maps; car okay to trailhead; 3.5 hours hiking time one way.

LOCATION: Douglas Ranger District - Chiricahua Mountains.

DIFFICULTY: Difficult

ELEVATIONS: 5360' - 8800'

LENGTH: 6.8 miles one way.

MAPS REQUIRED: U.S.G.S. 7.5 min. topographic for Portal Peak.

PERMIT: No

BIKES: No

EQUESTRIAN: Not recommended.

WATER: Yes - best to bring your own.

INFORMATION: You can add to this hike in many ways; study your maps.

FIREARMS: Yes

PETS ON LEASH: Yes

TRAIL INFORMATION

Take I-10 east from Tucson 140 miles, across the New Mexico border to U.S. 80 and turn right (south). Travel about 28 miles then turn right (west) on the road to Portal. From Portal travel south on Forest Road #42 to the South Fork turnoff. In about a mile will be the South Fork picnic area and trailhead.

About 1.5 miles into the trail will be Maple Camp which is a good example of a riparian location. Still climbing after Maple Camp, as well as following a nice stream, high cliffs become evident as you climb further into the canyon. As you continue to climb towards the end of your hike, you will pass Burnt Stump Trail #366 on your left. Turn right here and soon will be a junction with Crest Trail #270. A left turn here will take you to the summit of Sentinel Peak in only .5 mile of travel.

If not adding to your hike, return the same way.

SOUTH FORK TRAIL #243

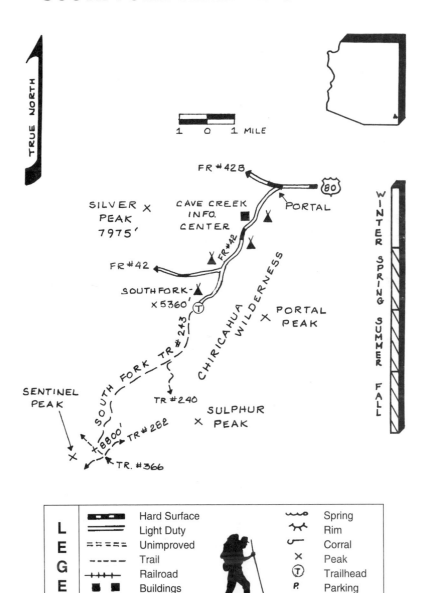

TRUE NORTH

1   0   1 MILE

WINTER SPRING SUMMER FALL

FR #42B

80

SILVER × PEAK 7975'

CAVE CREEK INFO. CENTER

PORTAL

FR #42

FR #42

SOUTH FORK 5360'

× 5360'

CHIRICAHUA WILDERNESS

PORTAL PEAK

SENTINEL PEAK

SOUTH FORK TR # 243

8800'

TR # 282

TR # 240

SULPHUR × PEAK

TR. #366

L E G E N D		
▬ ▬	Hard Surface	
▬▬▬	Light Duty	
= = = =	Unimproved	
- - - -	Trail	
+++++	Railroad	
■ ■	Buildings	
○	Water Tank	
▲	Campsite	
×5270	Elevation Check	

∿∿o	Spring
⤸	Rim
⌒	Corral
×	Peak
Ⓣ	Trailhead
P.	Parking
☁	Water
∿	River
∿...∿.	Drainage

ATASCOSA TRAIL #100

ATTRACTION: Solitude, nice views of Atascosa Peak and all other major mountains, as it is a 360-degree viewing area, including Mexico.

REQUIREMENTS: Food, water, sturdy boots, proper maps; car okay to trailhead; 3.5 hours hiking time round trip.

LOCATION: Nogales Ranger District - Atascosa Mountain.

DIFFICULTY: Difficult

ELEVATIONS: 4700' - 6250'

LENGTH: 2.5 miles one way

MAPS REQUIRED: U.S.G.S. 7.5 min. topographic for Ruby.

PERMIT: No

BIKES: No

EQUESTRIAN: Not recommended.

WATER: No - bring your own.

INFORMATION: Trail not well marked and rocky in some areas, a true test of your abilities.

FIREARMS: Yes

PETS ON LEASH: Yes

TRAIL INFORMATION

Take I-19 about 12 miles north of Nogales to the Peña Blanca/Ruby exit, then go west to Peña Blanca Lake. Watch carefully and by staying left you will pick up Forest Road #39. Stay on Forest Road #39 and, in just under 5 miles, you will come to the trailhead at a very small clearing on your left.

You will not hike long before you will encounter several switchbacks on your way to a gate at about the 1-mile mark. It will be interesting to observe all the different vegetation along the trail, from hot and dry to lichen-covered overhangs close to the end of the trail. You will finally scramble to the peak via an unmistakable rocky area on its west slope.

Return the same way.

ATASCOSA TRAIL #100

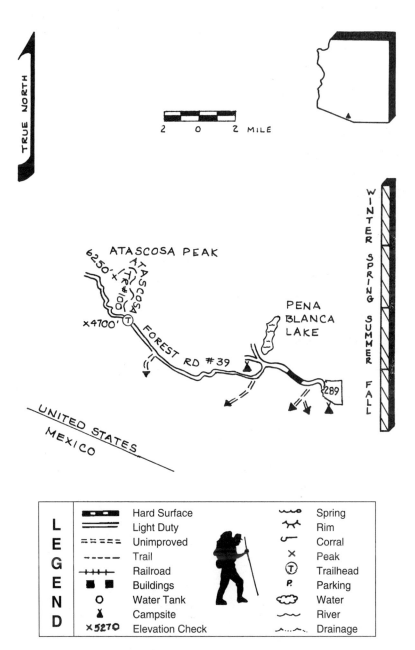

TRUE NORTH

2 0 2 MILE

WINTER SPRING SUMMER FALL

ATASCOSA PEAK

6250'
ATASCOSA TR #100

×4700'

FOREST RD #39

PENA BLANCA LAKE

289

UNITED STATES
MEXICO

LEGEND		
▬▬ Hard Surface		⌇⌇o Spring
══ Light Duty		⁀ Rim
═══ Unimproved		⌐ Corral
----- Trail		× Peak
┼┼┼ Railroad		Ⓣ Trailhead
■ ■ Buildings		P. Parking
o Water Tank		☁ Water
▲ Campsite		⌇ River
×5270 Elevation Check		⌁ Drainage

ARMOUR SPRING TRAIL #71

ATTRACTION: Nice secluded spot for a picnic lunch.

REQUIREMENTS: Food, water, sturdy boots, proper maps; car okay to trailhead for Florida Canyon Trail #145; 3/4 hour hiking time one way.

LOCATION: Nogales Ranger District - Santa Rita Mountains.

DIFFICULTY: Moderate

ELEVATIONS: 7920' - 8140'

LENGTH: .4 mile one way

MAPS REQUIRED: U.S.G.S. 7.5 min. topographic for Mt. Wrightson.

PERMIT: No

BIKES: No

EQUESTRIAN: Yes

WATER: Yes, but best to bring your own.

INFORMATION: Keep in mind there is a 5-mile hike one way to get to the trailhead; watch the weather.

FIREARMS: Yes

PETS ON LEASH: Yes

TRAIL INFORMATION

Follow all directions for Florida Canyon Trail #145 and first part of Crest Trail #144 to get to this trailhead.

This short, but interesting, trail takes you directly to Armour Spring via a nice, shady area.

This little-traveled area is a nice rest stop to snack, snooze or just enjoy the serenity.

Return the same way.

ARMOUR SPRING TRAIL #71

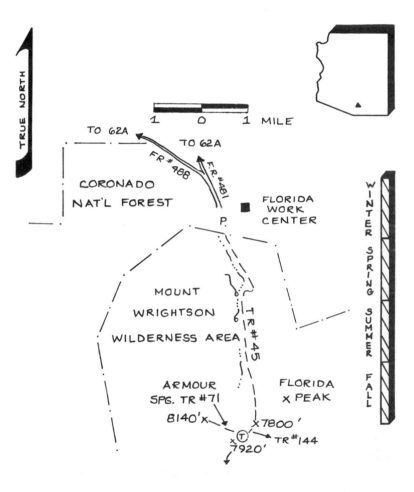

LEGEND		
▄▬▄ Hard Surface	⌣⌣o Spring
═══ Light Duty	⋌⋋ Rim
≅≅≅≅ Unimproved	⌒ Corral
----- Trail	✕ Peak
┼┼┼┼ Railroad	Ⓣ Trailhead
▀ ■ Buildings	P. Parking
o Water Tank	☁ Water
⚑ Campsite	∼ River
✕5270 Elevation Check	⌒...⌒. Drainage

BOG SPRINGS TRAIL #156

ATTRACTION: Secluded, short hike with good chance of many wildlife sightings, lots of shady picnic areas.

REQUIREMENTS: Food, water, sturdy boots, proper maps; car okay to trailhead; 1.5 hours hiking time one way.

LOCATION: Nogales Ranger District - Santa Rita Mountains.

DIFFICULTY: Moderate

ELEVATIONS: 4820' - 6620'

LENGTH: 2.7 miles one way.

MAPS REQUIRED: U.S.G.S. 7.5 min. topographic for Mt. Wrightson.

PERMIT: No

BIKES: No

EQUESTRIAN: Yes

WATER: Not dependable - bring your own.

INFORMATION: This trail, along with Kent Spring Trail #157, makes for an excellent 4.3-mile loop hike for the whole family.

FIREARMS: Yes   **PETS ON LEASH:** Yes

TRAIL INFORMATION

Take I-19 south from Tucson to the Continental/Madera Canyon Road. Follow Madera Canyon Road to Madera Canyon and Bog Springs Campground. The trailhead is found just past the third campsite on the right.

It begins as an old jeep trail no longer used, and is pretty much uphill right away. In just over .5 mile, you reach a saddle. At this point the trail takes off to the left and the jeep trail ends here. Soon an old mining area comes into view on your left.

At about 1.5 miles from the start, the lush area of Bog Springs appears. Next you travel gently up a draw and, after turning right, climb steeply, by way of some moderate switchbacks, to a welcome ridge with great views. Continuing now and still climbing, soon Kent Spring will appear at the 2.7-mile mark at trail's end.

You may return the way you came up or continue now on Kent Spring Trail #157 back to Bog Springs Campground.

BOG SPRINGS TRAIL #156

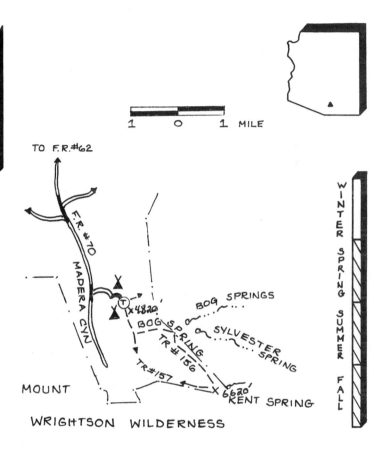

TRUE NORTH

1 0 1 MILE

TO F.R.#62

F.R.#70

MADERA CVN

TR#157

BOG SPRINGS

BOG SPRING
TR#156

SYLVESTER SPRING

X 4820

X 6620
KENT SPRING

MOUNT

WRIGHTSON WILDERNESS

WINTER SPRING SUMMER FALL

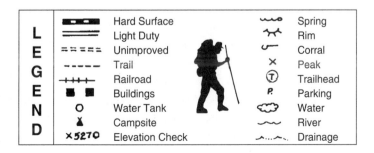

L E G E N D					
▬▬▬	Hard Surface		∿	Spring	
═══	Light Duty		⤴	Rim	
═ ═ ═	Unimproved		⌐	Corral	
- - - -	Trail		×	Peak	
+++++	Railroad		Ⓣ	Trailhead	
■ ■	Buildings		P.	Parking	
O	Water Tank		☁	Water	
▲	Campsite		∿	River	
×5270	Elevation Check		ᗨ...ᗨ	Drainage	

CREST TRAIL #144

ATTRACTION: Access to Mt. Wrightson (Old Baldy) at 9453', breathtaking views along the entire trail, abundance of plants and wildlife.

REQUIREMENTS: Food, water, sturdy boots, proper maps; car okay to the trailhead for Florida Canyon Trail #145; 2.5 hours hiking time one way.

LOCATION: Nogales Ranger District - Santa Rita Mountains.

DIFFICULTY: Moderate to Difficult.

ELEVATIONS: 7800' - 9453'

LENGTH: 3.2 miles one way.

MAPS REQUIRED: U.S.G.S. 7.5 min. topographic for Mt. Wrightson.

PERMIT: No

BIKES: No   **EQUESTRIAN:** Yes

WATER: Yes, but best to bring your own.

INFORMATION: 3.2 mile hike one way on Florida Canyon Trail #145 to the actual trailhead for Crest Trail #144; be very careful of the weather.

FIREARMS: Yes   **PETS ON LEASH:** Yes

TRAIL INFORMATION

Follow all directions to Florida Canyon Trail #145, as well as the trail itself, to the trailhead of Crest Trail #144.

Actual trailhead is at the end of Florida Canyon Trail at an intersection of sorts, where East Sawmill Canyon Trail #146 heads downhill to the northeast. Bear right here and, in a very short distance, a spur trail heads northwest called Armour Spring Trail #71 (see description of Armour Spring Trail #71). Bear left here and continue.

Crest Trail soon connects with Super Trail #134 and Old Baldy Trail #372 to Mt. Wrightson peak at 9453'. The upper portion of this trail is well traveled so you should have no trouble finding your way to the peak, where the Gulf of California can be seen on a clear day.

Return the same way or study your map to build on your hike.

CREST TRAIL #144

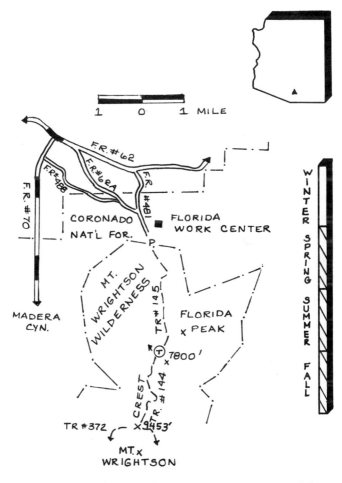

TRUE NORTH

1 0 1 MILE

WINTER SPRING SUMMER FALL

F.R. #62

F.R. #62A

F.R. #481

F.R. #488

F.R. #70

CORONADO NAT'L FOR.

FLORIDA WORK CENTER

P

MT. WRIGHTSON WILDERNESS

TR #145

MADERA CYN.

FLORIDA x PEAK

Ⓣ 7800'

CREST TR. #144

TR #372

x9453'

MT. x WRIGHTSON

L	▬ ▪ ▬	Hard Surface	∽ ○	Spring	
E	═══	Light Duty	∼∼	Rim	
	= = = =	Unimproved	⌐	Corral	
G	- - - -	Trail	×	Peak	
E	┼┼┼┼	Railroad	Ⓣ	Trailhead	
N	▪ ▪	Buildings	P.	Parking	
	○	Water Tank	⌒⌒	Water	
D	▲	Campsite	∼∼	River	
	×5270	Elevation Check	∼...∼.	Drainage	

DUTCH JOHN TRAIL #91

ATTRACTION: A very shaded hike with excellent chances for wildlife sightings, as well as a riparian habitat.

REQUIREMENTS: Food, water, sturdy boots, proper maps; car okay to trailhead; 1.5 hours hiking time one way.

LOCATION: Nogales Ranger District - Santa Rita Mountains.

DIFFICULTY: Moderate to Difficult

ELEVATIONS: 4820' - 6020'

LENGTH: 1.8 miles one way.

MAPS REQUIRED: U.S.G.S. 7.5 min. topographic for Mt. Wrightson.

PERMIT: No

BIKES: No

EQUESTRIAN: Yes

WATER: Yes, but purify.

INFORMATION: This is bear country!

FIREARMS: Yes

PETS ON LEASH: Yes

TRAIL INFORMATION

Take I-19 south out of Tucson to the Continental/Madera Canyon exit. Follow Madera Canyon Road to Bog Springs Campground, a distance of a little under 13 miles. The trailhead is in the rear of the campground.

Trail starts uphill right away under a canopy of shade and takes you in and out of several drainages. Shortly, you drop into Dutch John Canyon and then you start to climb again, passing through an area containing your first spring. Continue through this area to a second spring and trail's end.

This is a nice area to take a nap and let the world go by.

Return the way you came.

DUTCH JOHN TRAIL #91

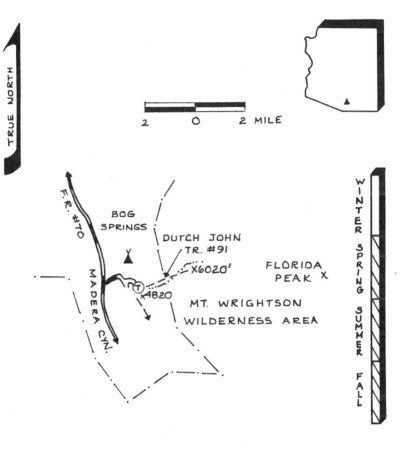

TRUE NORTH

2 0 2 MILE

WINTER SPRING SUMMER FALL

F.R. #70

BOG SPRINGS

MADERA CYN.

DUTCH JOHN TR. #91

X6020'

T X4820

FLORIDA PEAK X

MT. WRIGHTSON WILDERNESS AREA

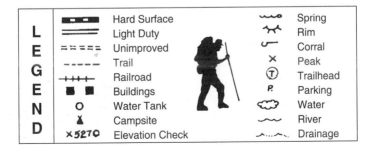

LEGEND				
	Hard Surface		Spring	
	Light Duty		Rim	
	Unimproved		Corral	
	Trail	×	Peak	
	Railroad	Ⓣ	Trailhead	
	Buildings	P.	Parking	
o	Water Tank		Water	
⚱	Campsite		River	
×5270	Elevation Check		Drainage	

FLORIDA CANYON TRAIL #145

ATTRACTION: Fantastic views, access to many trails, uncrowded, wild flowers in season.

REQUIREMENTS: Food, water, sturdy boots, proper maps; car okay to trailhead; 3 hours hiking time one way.

LOCATION: Nogales Ranger District - Santa Rita Mountains.

DIFFICULTY: Moderate to Difficult.

ELEVATIONS: 4340' - 7800'

LENGTH: 4.6 miles one way.

MAPS REQUIRED: U.S.G.S. 7.5 min. topographic for Mt. Wrightson.

PERMIT: No

BIKES: No

EQUESTRIAN: Yes

WATER: Yes, but best to bring your own.

INFORMATION: Don't let the distant views keep luring you deeper into this area unless you are prepared.

FIREARMS: Yes

PETS ON LEASH: Yes

TRAIL INFORMATION

Take I-19 south of Tucson to the Continental/Madera Canyon Road exit. Follow the Madera Canyon Road just under 7.5 miles to Forest Road #62. Watch very closely for Forest Road #62A and make a right turn. Follow Forest Road #62A a little over 3.5 miles to the trailhead; it will be on your left.

Very little explanation is needed to follow this trail as it and the others, to which you will have access, are clearly marked. You will see endless varieties of plants and wildlife, as well as geological formations of every kind. Stunning views await you.

Return the same way or study your maps to build on this hike.

FLORIDA CANYON
TRAIL #145

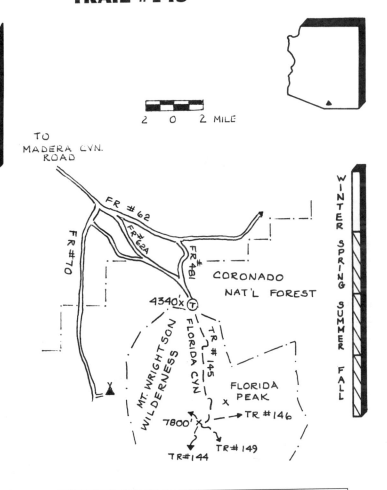

TRUE NORTH

2 0 2 MILE

WINTER SPRING SUMMER FALL

TO
MADERA CVN.
ROAD

FR #62

FR #62A

FR #70

FR #481

CORONADO
NAT'L FOREST

4340'x (T)

MT. WRIGHTSON WILDERNESS

FLORIDA CVN

TR #145

FLORIDA
PEAK
x

→ TR #146

7800' x

TR #149

TR #144

L	▬ ▭ ▬	Hard Surface	⌇⌇o Spring
E	══════	Light Duty	Rim
G	═ ═ ═ ═ ═	Unimproved	⌐ Corral
	- - - - -	Trail	× Peak
E	┼┼┼┼┼	Railroad	Ⓣ Trailhead
N	■ ■	Buildings	P. Parking
	o	Water Tank	⟅⟆ Water
D	⚑	Campsite	River
	×5270	Elevation Check	Drainage

LEGEND

KENT SPRING TRAIL #157

ATTRACTION: Secluded, short hike with good chance of many wildlife sightings, lots of shady picnic areas.

REQUIREMENTS: Food, water, sturdy boots, proper maps; car okay to Bog Springs Trail #156 trailhead; 1 hour hiking time one way.

LOCATION: Nogales Ranger District - Santa Rita Mountains.

DIFFICULTY: Moderate

ELEVATIONS: 5080' - 6620'

LENGTH: 1.6 miles one way.

MAPS REQUIRED: U.S.G.S. 7.5 min. topographic for Mt. Wrightson.

PERMIT: No

BIKES: No

EQUESTRIAN: Yes

WATER: Not dependable - bring your own.

INFORMATION: This trail, along with Bog Springs Trail #156, make for an excellent 4.3-mile loop hike for the whole family.

FIREARMS: Yes

PETS ON LEASH: Yes

TRAIL INFORMATION

You will find the upper trailhead for this trail at Kent Spring. Follow directions for Bog Springs Trail #156 to arrive at Kent Spring.

You will not find Kent Spring as shaded as Bog Springs, but the water is usually dependable. Leaving here, you quickly lose altitude for .5 mile to Sylvester Spring, the least impressive of the three.

After climbing a draw on your left and dropping down through a drainage ditch leading to Madera Creek, the trail makes its way to a fork. Although there are no signs, you must stay to the right and, at just over 4 miles from the start (Bog Springs Campground), you will find yourself back at the saddle. Turn right and continue back to Bog Springs Campground via the old jeep trail.

KENT SPRING TRAIL #157

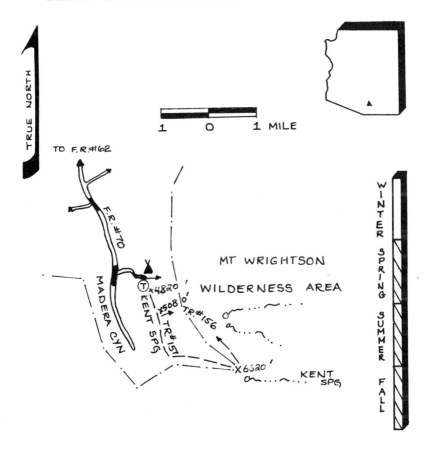

TRUE NORTH

1   0   1 MILE

TO F.R.#62

F.R.#70

MADERA CYN

MT WRIGHTSON

WILDERNESS AREA

T ×4820

KENT SPG

×508

×5270

TR.#157

TR.#156

×6520

KENT SPG

WINTER SPRING SUMMER FALL

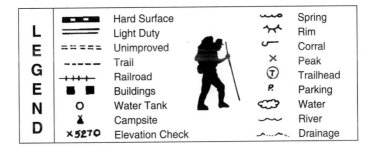

L E G E N D					
	▬▬▬	Hard Surface		∿∿o	Spring
	═══	Light Duty		↭	Rim
	═ ═ ═	Unimproved		↶	Corral
	- - - -	Trail		×	Peak
	+++++	Railroad		Ⓣ	Trailhead
	■ ■	Buildings		P.	Parking
	○	Water Tank		☁	Water
	⚑	Campsite		∿	River
	×5270	Elevation Check		∿...∿.	Drainage

OLD BALDY TRAIL #372

ATTRACTION: Fantastic views, bird watcher's paradise, views of Gulf of California and San Francisco Peaks on clear day.

REQUIREMENTS: Food, water, sturdy boots, proper maps; car okay to trailhead; 8-9 hours hiking time round trip.

LOCATION: Nogales Ranger District, 38 miles south of Tucson.

DIFFICULTY: Difficult

ELEVATIONS: 5440' - 8760'

LENGTH: 8.4 miles round trip to Baldy Saddle.

MAPS REQUIRED: U.S.G.S. 15 min. topographic for Mt. Wrightson.

PERMIT: No

BIKES: No

EQUESTRIAN: Yes

WATER: Not dependable.

INFORMATION: Trail very steep in some spots; know your limits. Great loop trail using Super Trail #134 coming down.

FIREARMS: Yes

PETS ON LEASH: Yes

TRAIL INFORMATION

Follow trailhead directions from Super Trail #134 to Roundup Campground and park. On a dirt road .3 mile south of the parking lot is the trailhead junction for Old Baldy Trail #372 and Treasure Vault Trail #77. Some of the canyon walls rise 1500' above your head. You will pass a helispot at 1.7 miles with nice views and undeveloped campsites at 2 miles. At Josephine Saddle, 2.2 miles, are 4 trails: Agua Caliente #140, Josephine #133, Old Baldy #372 and Super Trail #134. All trails in the Santa Rita Mountains can be accessed from here. Old Baldy and Super Trail become one for .2 mile. You will pass Temporal Trail #595 at 2.3 miles. At 2.4 miles Old Baldy and Super Trail split.

After winding along the north side of the canyon and at the end of a series of switchbacks there is a campsite and good views. Bellow Springs is just .1 mile more. From the spring to Baldy

(Continued on Page 48)

OLD BALDY TRAIL #372

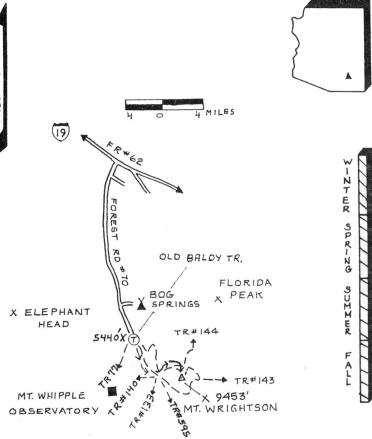

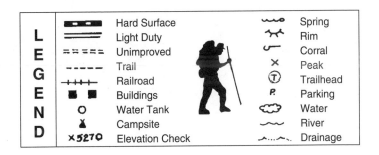

(Continued from Page 46)

Saddle at 4.2 miles is a .7 mile 15-20% uphill grade. There are good views of Mt. Hopkins and its telescopes from here. Old Baldy and Super Trail again become one and intersect with Crest Trail #144 which heads north.

The last mile to the top gets much steeper with a lot of switchbacks and loose rock. Pace yourself; *altitude sickness can set in easily here.* Old Baldy Trail ends at Baldy Saddle. The last mile to the top is Super Trail #134.

Mt. Wrightson (Old Baldy) at sunset.
(Photo by John Villinski)

The final push to Baldy Saddle.
(Photo by John Villinski)

The view south from Baldy Saddle.
(Photo by John Villinski)

SUPER TRAIL #134

ATTRACTION: Fantastic views, bird watcher's paradise.

REQUIREMENTS: Food, water, sturdy boots, proper maps; car okay to trailhead; 8-9 hours hiking time round trip.

LOCATION: Nogales Ranger District, 38 miles south of Tucson.

DIFFICULTY: Difficult

ELEVATIONS: 5440' - 9453'

LENGTH: 8.1 miles one way.

MAPS REQUIRED: U.S.G.S. 15 min. topographic for Mt. Wrightson.

PERMIT: No

BIKES: No

EQUESTRIAN: Yes

WATER: Not dependable - bring your own.

INFORMATION: Weather very unpredictable on summit any time of year; time your hike correctly; pace yourself.

FIREARMS: Yes   **PETS ON LEASH:** Yes

TRAIL INFORMATION

Travel south of Tucson on I-19 and exit at the Continental turnoff (#63). After a left turn here, watch for another left turn onto White House Canyon Road. Then 12 miles later, turn onto Madera Canyon Road and park at Roundup Campground picnic area. Trail leaves the parking area along a drainage.

From here, the trail continues 8.1 miles to the top with its relentless 8% grade. Trail difficulty is rated as fair, but at times it seems much worse as there is no letup in the grade anywhere.

At the halfway point, you will arrive at Josephine Saddle where four trails converge. Continue on Super Trai #134. From this point on, the trail switchbacks become more numerous to Baldy Saddle at 7.1 miles. To this point you will have traversed about 75 switchbacks. The last mile to the top gets much steeper, with about 39 more switchbacks, so pace yourself; you're almost there. *Altitude sick-ness can set in easily here.*

On a clear day, the Gulf of California can be seen from the rounded 50 by 200 foot peak of Mt. Wrightson.

SUPER TRAIL #134

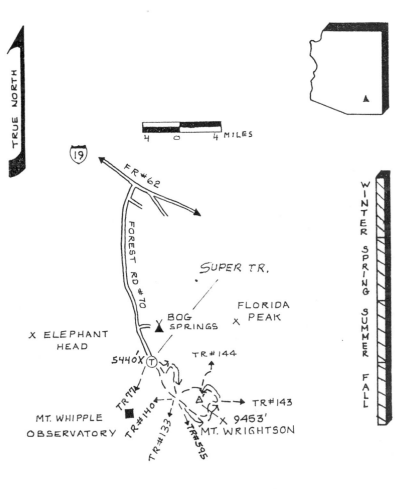

TRUE NORTH

(19)
FR #62

FOREST RD #70

SUPER TR.

BOG SPRINGS

FLORIDA PEAK

X ELEPHANT HEAD

5440X (T)

TR #144

TR 77A

TR #143

MT. WHIPPLE OBSERVATORY

TR #140

TR #133

TR #595

X 9453' MT. WRIGHTSON

WINTER SPRING SUMMER FALL

4   0   4 MILES

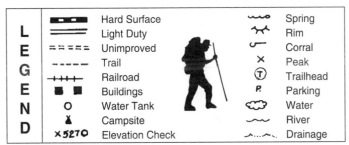

L	▬▬▬	Hard Surface	∿o	Spring
E	═══	Light Duty	⌣⌣	Rim
	═════	Unimproved	⌐	Corral
G	-----	Trail	×	Peak
E	┼┼┼┼	Railroad	(T)	Trailhead
N	■ ■	Buildings	P.	Parking
	O	Water Tank	⌒⌒	Water
D	⚑	Campsite	∼	River
	×5270	Elevation Check	∼…∼	Drainage

SYCAMORE CANYON TRAIL #40

ATTRACTION: Unusual wildlife, canyon hiking which is always a challenge—this trail will test your limits for sure.

REQUIREMENTS: Food, water, sturdy boots, proper maps; car not recommended to trailhead; 4-6 hours hiking time one way.

LOCATION: Nogales Ranger District - Peña Blanca Lake area.

DIFFICULTY: Most difficult

ELEVATIONS: 5000'- 3500'

LENGTH: 5.3 miles one way.

MAPS REQUIRED: U.S.G.S. 7.5 min. topographic for Ruby.

PERMIT: No

BIKES: No

EQUESTRIAN: Not recommended.

WATER: Yes - best to bring your own or purify

INFORMATION: Latter part very rocky and, at times, there is no trail. The terrain discourages many; know your limits. Flash flooding possible.

FIREARMS: Yes

PETS ON LEASH: Yes

TRAIL INFORMATION

From I-19, 12 miles north of Nogales, turn west at the Peña Blanca-Ruby Road exit. Stay on paved road approximately 9 miles to Peña Blanca Recreation Area. At this point you will leave the pavement and follow Arivaca-Ruby Road for 8.5 miles to Sycamore Canyon Road #218. Turn left and travel 1/4 mile to the Hank and Yank Ruins historical marker; park here.

The first 1 1/4 mile is easy although it is 1 - 1 1/2 hours hiking time one way to this point. The trail is very difficult from this point on as it requires one to find his or her own way much of the time; the idea is to follow the canyon. You will know the end of the trail when you come to a fence across the canyon just over 5 miles from the trailhead. This marks the U.S./Mexico border—go no further!

NOTE: No camping is allowed in Sycamore Canyon below the Hank and Yank Ruins.

SYCAMORE CANYON
TRAIL #40

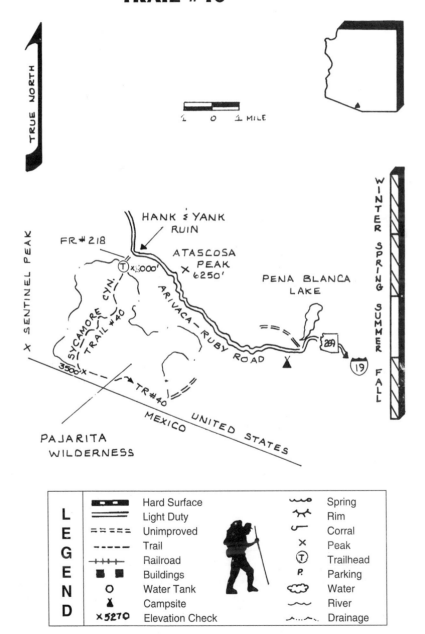

1   0   1 MILE

TRUE NORTH

WINTER SPRING SUMMER FALL

HANK & YANK RUIN

FR #218

ATASCOSA PEAK ×6250'

X SENTINEL PEAK

T ×5000'

PENA BLANCA LAKE

SYCAMORE CYN. TRAIL #40

ARIVACA-RUBY ROAD

289

19

3500'×

TR #40

MEXICO   UNITED STATES

PAJARITA WILDERNESS

L	▬▬▬	Hard Surface	◡◡○	Spring
E	═══	Light Duty	⋏⋏⋏	Rim
G	═ ═ ═ ═ ═	Unimproved	◡	Corral
E	-----	Trail	×	Peak
N	++++++	Railroad	Ⓣ	Trailhead
D	▬ ▬	Buildings	P.	Parking
	○	Water Tank	☁	Water
	✗	Campsite	◡◡	River
	×5270	Elevation Check	◡...◡.	Drainage

BEAR CANYON TRAIL #29

ATTRACTION: At 2.2 miles is Seven Falls side trip; study your map for other trail possibilities.

REQUIREMENTS: Food, water, sturdy boots, proper maps; car okay to Sabino Canyon Visitor Ctr.; 4 hours hiking time one way.

LOCATION: Santa Catalina Ranger District - Santa Catalina Mountains, Tucson.

DIFFICULTY: Easy to Moderate

ELEVATIONS: 2800' - 4800' - 3680'

LENGTH: 8.6 miles one way.

MAPS REQUIRED: Santa Catalina Mountain Trail and Recreation map, basic 15 minute series, U.S. Forest Service

PERMIT: No   **BIKES:** No

EQUESTRIAN: Moderate   **WATER:** Not dependable

INFORMATION: Either walk 1.7 miles to trailhead or take tram from Sabino Canyon Visitor Center.

FIREARMS: No   **PETS ON LEASH:** No

TRAIL INFORMATION

Trailhead can be reached by taking the tram from the Sabino Canyon Visitor Center for just under 2 miles. The trail skirts Bear Creek for first 2 miles. You will cross the creek several times via handmade stepping stones. As the massive cliffs close in on you, you will come to a couple of switchbacks which take the trail to about 100' above the creek. At about 2 miles, a small trail takes off to the left for .2 mile leading to Seven Falls, well worth seeing during wet periods. Bear Canyon Trail #29 continues to the right.

Trail continues up the canyon above the creek (nice view of the falls). After crossing creek, prepare for some switchbacking. Trail now gets easier and continues to an old intersection at Thimble Saddle. The correct trail is obvious, to the left.

Trail is mostly downhill now and very distinct for the next mile where Pine Creek and the Palisade trailhead are located. Palisade Trail is to the right; continue straight. It is a mile to the trail's end but, just before the Box Camp Trail, it turns right. At the main intersection, Phone Line Trail is to the left and West Fork Sabino Trail is to the right.

BEAR CANYON TRAIL #29

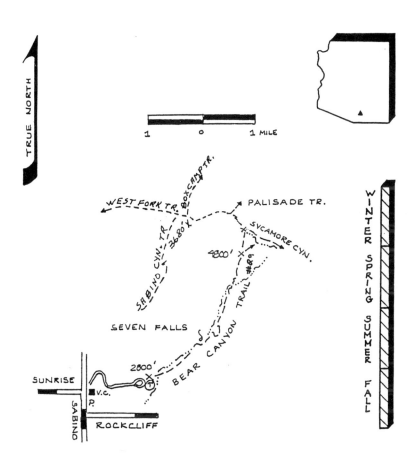

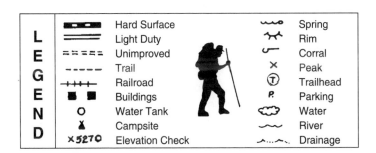

BUTTERFLY TRAIL #16

ATTRACTION: Unusual varieties of plant growth; nice views.

REQUIREMENTS: Food, water, sturdy boots, proper maps; car okay to trailhead; 3 hours hiking time one way.

LOCATION: Santa Catalina Ranger District - Santa Catalina Mountains, Tucson.

DIFFICULTY: Moderate to Difficult

ELEVATIONS: 7680' - 8350' - 7950'

LENGTH: 5.7 miles one way.

MAPS REQUIRED: Santa Catalina Mountain Trail and Recreation map, basic 15 minute series, U.S. Forest Service.

PERMIT: No   **BIKES:** Yes

EQUESTRIAN: Moderate - some narrow areas.

WATER: Yes, except during dry months.

INFORMATION: Connects Soldier Camp with Palisade Ranger Station.

FIREARMS: Yes   **PETS ON LEASH:** Yes

TRAIL INFORMATION

Trailhead is at the gravel road turnoff to Soldier Camp from the Mt. Lemmon Highway. The trail starts out on this road and follows it for about .2 mile just before it turns into a regular foot trail.

From here to Crystal Spring Trail #17 intersection, at the 1.4 mile mark, is a section with a fair amount of altitude loss. At this intersection, Crystal Spring is to the left; continue straight.

For the next 1.8 miles, you traverse some switchbacks to about the Novio Spring area and lose about 300' in altitude, only to gain it and more back from the spring to the Davis Spring Trail intersection. Davis Spring is to the left; continue straight.

The next section of trail (2 miles) is the most difficult with over a 1200' altitude gain to a saddle just east of the Mt. Bigelow Towers. At this intersection the radio towers, Mt. Bigelow and the fire tower are to your right. From here, continue straight for next .5 mile as trail drops down to end of trail at Palisade Ranger Station on Mt. Lemmon Highway. Return the way you came or arrange a shuttle.

BUTTERFLY TRAIL #16

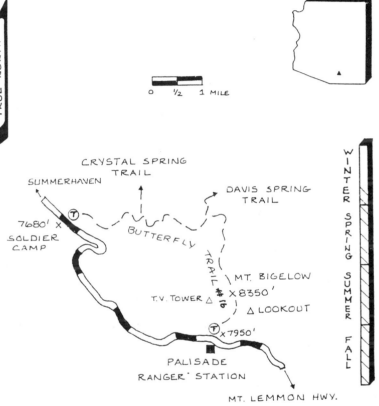

TRUE NORTH

0   ½   1 MILE

CRYSTAL SPRING TRAIL

SUMMERHAVEN

DAVIS SPRING TRAIL

7680' X
SOLDIER CAMP

BUTTERFLY TRAIL

MT. BIGELOW X 8350'

T.V. TOWER △

△ LOOKOUT

X 7950'

PALISADE RANGER STATION

MT. LEMMON HWY.

WINTER SPRING SUMMER FALL

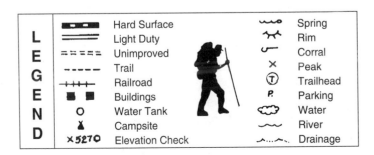

▬ ▬ ▭	Hard Surface	∿o	Spring
═══	Light Duty	⌃⌃⌃	Rim
═ ═ ═══	Unimproved	↶	Corral
-----	Trail	×	Peak
┼┼┼┼	Railroad	Ⓣ	Trailhead
■ ■	Buildings	P.	Parking
O	Water Tank	❀	Water
⚑	Campsite	⌁	River
×5270	Elevation Check	⌁...⌁	Drainage

L E G E N D

CRYSTAL SPRING TRAIL #17

ATTRACTION: At the top is an area covered with a lot of tall ferns.

REQUIREMENTS: Food, water, sturdy boots, proper maps; high clearance vehicle to trailhead; 2 hours hiking time one way.

LOCATION: Santa Catalina Ranger District - Santa Catalina Mountains.

DIFFICULTY: Moderate

ELEVATIONS: 6400' - 7060'

LENGTH: 3.6 miles one way

MAPS REQUIRED: Santa Catalina Mountain Trail and Recreation Map.

PERMIT: No

BIKES: Yes

EQUESTRIAN: Yes, but there are narrow sections.

WATER: Yes, but best to bring your own.

INFORMATION: Travels from a point along Mt. Lemmon Highway to Butterfly Trail #16.

FIREARMS: Yes

PETS ON LEASH: Yes

TRAIL INFORMATION

Traveling on the Mt. Lemmon Highway, north of Summerhaven start watching for the Oracle-Mt. Lemmon Road in a little over 3 miles. Take this road and watch for a trail sign just before a long switchback in just under 3 miles.

As you begin your moderate ascent, several drainages are encountered before arriving in Alder Canyon. Now, on a side wall in Alder Canyon below you, you will notice a wooden water trough in a fenced area (Crystal Spring). Still moderately climbing, you will reach a very flat, grassy area begging you to stay around awhile, and maybe enjoy your lunch now that your worst climbs are over.

Soon you arrive at the junction of Butterfly Trail ##16. A right turn here takes you to Soldier Camp in 1.5 miles. A left turn takes you to Palisade Ranger Station in a little over 4 miles.

A car shuttle works nicely.

CRYSTAL SPRING TRAIL #17

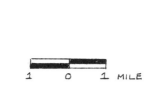

1   0   1   MILE

TRUE NORTH

WINTER SPRING SUMMER FALL

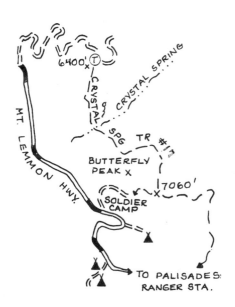

6400'× (T)

CRYSTAL SPRING

CRYSTAL

SPG   TR   #17

MT. LEMMON HWY.

BUTTERFLY
PEAK ×

7060'
×

SOLDIER
CAMP

TO PALISADES
RANGER STA.

L E G E N D			
▬▬▬	Hard Surface	∿o	Spring
═══	Light Duty	⋎⋎	Rim
═ ═ ═	Unimproved	ʊ	Corral
- - - -	Trail	×	Peak
┼┼┼┼	Railroad	(T)	Trailhead
■ ■	Buildings	P.	Parking
O	Water Tank	⊂⊃	Water
▲	Campsite	∿	River
×5270	Elevation Check	∿...∿.	Drainage

ITALIAN SPRING TRAIL #95

ATTRACTION: Shortest way to Manning Camp.

REQUIREMENTS: Food, water, very sturdy boots, maps; high profile 4-wheel drive to trailhead; 3.5 hours hiking time one way.

LOCATION: Santa Catalina Ranger District - Saguaro National Monument East - Rincon Mountains.

DIFFICULTY: Difficult

ELEVATIONS: 4000' - 6780'   **LENGTH:** 3.2 miles one way.

MAPS REQUIRED: U.S.G.S. 7.5 min. topographic for Agua Caliente, Piety Hill, Mica Mountain.

PERMIT: Permit needed if camping overnight, issued from Saguaro National Monument East.

BIKES: No   **EQUESTRIAN:** Difficult

WATER: Not dependable

INFORMATION: 3-hour trip from Tucson to get to trailhead (4-wheel drive); 2.5 miles of hike in Rincon Wilderness.

FIREARMS: No   **PETS ON LEASH:** No

TRAIL INFORMATION

Access to Italian Spring trailhead is gained only by 4-wheel drive. Head east out of Tucson on Tanque Verde Road which turns into a dirt road—Reddington Pass Road. From this point to the Italian Spring turnoff is 9.6 miles. This turnoff is not marked; watch your odometer. Turn right and travel 5 more miles to the trailhead.

It will save a lot of brutal wear and tear on your 4-wheel drive if, after 2.1 of the 5 miles, you park and hike the rest of the way. This area is marked by a large fresh-water tank and a windmill and is called Italian Trap. From here it is only a 2.9-mile hike to the trailhead sign for Italian Spring Trail on very rough road.

From the trailhead it is 2.3 miles to the Saguaro National Monument boundary, and another 2.5 miles to North Slope Trail at the end. There is no letup on this trail as it is all uphill—be prepared for it. From trail's end it is not far to Manning Camp, a good place to spend the night.

ITALIAN SPRING TRAIL #95

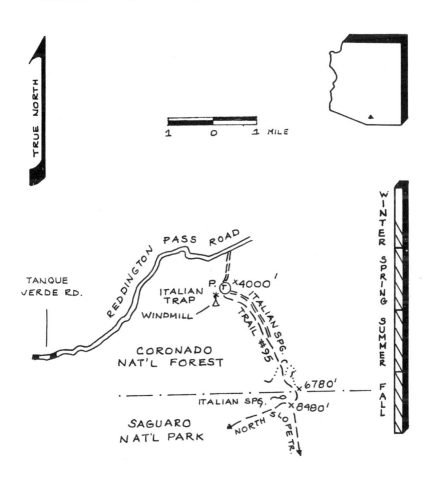

TRUE NORTH

1 0 1 MILE

WINTER SPRING SUMMER FALL

PASS ROAD

REDDINGTON

TANQUE VERDE RD.

ITALIAN TRAP

WINDMILL

P. (T) ×4000'

ITALIAN SPG. TRAIL #95

CORONADO NAT'L FOREST

×6780'

ITALIAN SPG.

×8480'

SAGUARO NAT'L PARK

NORTH SLOPE TR.

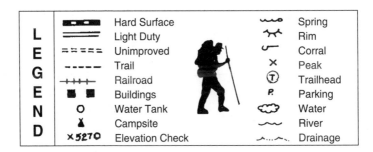

L	▬·▬·▬	Hard Surface	ᨦᨦ	Spring
E	════	Light Duty	⩙	Rim
G	⩵⩵⩵⩵	Unimproved	↵	Corral
	-----	Trail	×	Peak
G	⧻⧻⧻⧻	Railroad	(T)	Trailhead
E	■ ■	Buildings	P.	Parking
N	○	Water Tank	☁	Water
D	♟	Campsite	〜	River
	×5270○	Elevation Check	⌁...⌁.	Drainage

LEGEND

MARSHALL GULCH TRAIL #3

ATTRACTION: Very shady, secluded hike along Lemmon Creek enroute to Marshall Saddle from Marshall Gulch Campground.

REQUIREMENTS: Food, water, sturdy boots, proper maps; car okay to trailhead; 3/4 hour hiking time one way.

LOCATION: Santa Catalina Ranger District - Santa Catalina Mountains.

DIFFICULTY: Moderate

ELEVATIONS: 7280' - 8000'   **LENGTH:** 1.2 miles one way.

MAPS REQUIRED: Santa Catalina Mountain Trail and Recreation Map.

PERMIT: No   **BIKES:** No

EQUESTRIAN: Yes

WATER: Yes, but best to bring your own.

INFORMATION: Shortest way to Wilderness of Rocks geological area.

FIREARMS: Yes   **PETS ON LEASH:** No

TRAIL INFORMATION

High above Tucson on the Mt. Lemmon Highway, you will come to a fork in the road leading to Ski Valley on the right, and through the tiny village of Summerhaven to the left; take the left fork. In another mile you will arrive at the Marshall Gulch picnic area. Trail starts northwest out of the campground right beside a small building.

By taking Marshall Gulch Trail #3 for 1.2 miles, a lot of shade is to be enjoyed as you make your way along Lemmon Creek to Marshall Saddle. You may get confused shortly after the start, as there is a lower and an upper trail. They both join later but the upper trail will save you a sharp climb.

Trail will end at the sunny Marshall Saddle. At this trail junction, a right turn on Aspen Trail will head towards the ski area and a left turn on Aspen Trail will head back down to Marshall Gulch Campground, a nice loop hike. If you continue straight at the junction, the Wilderness of Rocks Trail #44 will take you into a very unique geological area.

MARSHALL GULCH TRAIL #3

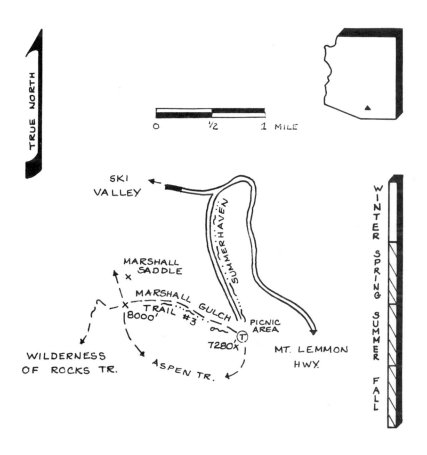

TRUE NORTH

0   ½   1 MILE

SKI VALLEY

WINTER SPRING SUMMER FALL

SUMMERHAVEN

MARSHALL SADDLE
x

MARSHALL GULCH
TRAIL #3
x
8000'

WILDERNESS OF ROCKS TR.

ASPEN TR.

PICNIC AREA

7280x (T)

MT. LEMMON HWY.

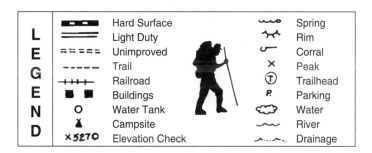

L E G E N D		
▬▬▬▬	Hard Surface	
═══════	Light Duty	
═ ═ ═ ═	Unimproved	
- - - - -	Trail	
++++++	Railroad	
▪ ▪	Buildings	
o	Water Tank	
✗	Campsite	
✗5270	Elevation Check	

∿o	Spring
⋏⋏	Rim
∽	Corral
×	Peak
(T)	Trailhead
P.	Parking
☁	Water
∿	River
⌒...⌒.	Drainage

MEADOW TRAIL #5A

ATTRACTION: Extremely nice area to picnic with entire family.

REQUIREMENTS: Snack, water, proper maps; car okay to trailhead; .5 hour hiking time one way.

LOCATION: Santa Catalina Ranger District - Santa Catalina Mountains.

DIFFICULTY: Easy

ELEVATIONS: 9050' - 8800'

LENGTH: 1 mile one way.

MAPS REQUIRED: Santa Catalina Mountain Trail and Recreation Map.

PERMIT: No

BIKES: Yes

EQUESTRIAN: Yes

WATER: Bring your own.

INFORMATION: You can drive within .5 mile of picnic area.

FIREARMS: Yes

PETS ON LEASH: Yes

TRAIL INFORMATION

Take the Mt. Lemmon Highway out of Tucson all the way to the Infrared Observatory atop Mt. Lemmon. Just east of the observatory is a road (paved) joined by an old service road that follows the Trico electric line; park here.

Note a fence surrounding the observatory. Head west from the southwest corner of this area, and in only minutes you will encounter a ridge and the trail will veer south along this ridge. You will enter Lemmon Park midway through the hike. It's an area almost too good to be true for a picnic, in spite of the lack of water.

Remainder of trail finally descends via switchbacks to its end at the junction of Mt. Lemmon Trail. Return the way you came.

MEADOW TRAIL #5A

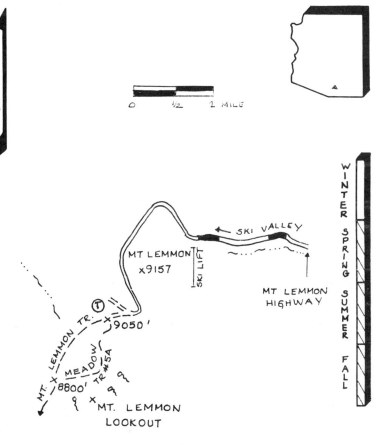

TRUE NORTH

0   1/2   1 MILE

WINTER SPRING SUMMER FALL

SKI VALLEY

MT LEMMON
x9157

SKI LIFT

MT LEMMON
HIGHWAY

MT. LEMMON TR.

9050'

MEADOW TR #5A

8800'

MT. LEMMON
LOOKOUT

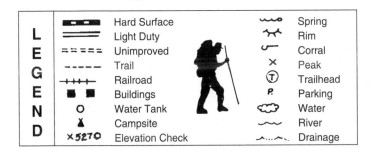

L E G E N D			
Hard Surface		Spring	
Light Duty		Rim	
Unimproved		Corral	
Trail		Peak	
Railroad		Trailhead	
Buildings		Parking	
O Water Tank		Water	
Campsite		River	
x5270 Elevation Check		Drainage	

MOUNT LEMMON TRAIL #5

ATTRACTION: Hutch's Pool and on to the third highest peak in Southern Arizona; fantastic panorama.

REQUIREMENTS: Food, water, sturdy boots, proper maps; check for all possible ways to access this trail via maps; 4 hours hiking time one way.

LOCATION: Santa Catalina Ranger District - Santa Catalina Mountains, Tucson.

DIFFICULTY: Moderate to Difficult

ELEVATIONS: 6100' - 9010'

LENGTH: 5.8 miles one way.

MAPS REQUIRED: Santa Catalina Mountain Trail and Recreation map, basic 15 minute series, U.S. Forest Service.

PERMIT: No   **BIKES:** No

EQUESTRIAN: Moderate to Difficult.

WATER: Yes - purify; should bring own.

INFORMATION: This trail not for a novice; do not attempt this trail unless in excellent condition; be well supplied.

FIREARMS: Yes   **PETS ON LEASH:** Yes

TRAIL INFORMATION

Trailhead is located at the intersection of Romero Canyon Trail and West Fork Trail west of Sabino Basin. It is a true introduction to the high country.

At this point, you are just over halfway to the top. A left turn would eventually drop you into Catalina State Park; continue to the right. Trail climbs moderately via a few switchbacks for the next 1.9 miles. Views here are almost second to none. Soon you arrive at the next intersection and the Wilderness of Rocks Trail to the right with all of its creations; continue to the left. Still climbing, the next 2.4 miles take you to the Cañada Del Oro Trail intersection and an old road. Sutherland, Samaniego Ridge and Cañada Del Oro Trails are to your left. Continue to the right on a service road past Lemmon Park Trail and Lemmon Rock Trail. Remain on road to summit, the highest point in the Catalinas. It works well to have a car here or arrange to be picked up. Consult your map.

MOUNT LEMMON TRAIL #5

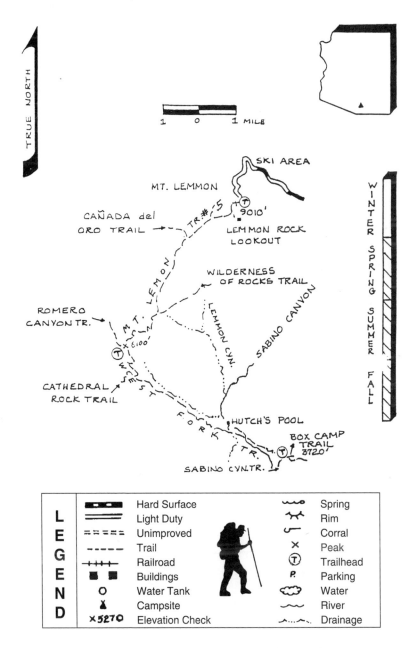

TRUE NORTH

1 0 1 MILE

WINTER SPRING SUMMER FALL

SKI AREA

MT. LEMMON

CAÑADA del
ORO TRAIL →

TR #5

(T)
9010'

LEMMON ROCK
LOOKOUT

WILDERNESS
OF ROCKS TRAIL

ROMERO
CANYON TR.

M T. LEMMON

×6100

SABINO CANYON

LEMMON CYN.

CATHEDRAL
ROCK TRAIL

WEST FORK

HUTCH'S POOL

BOX CAMP
TRAIL
3720'

(T)

SABINO CVNTR.

L E G E N D		
▬▬▬ Hard Surface		⌣○ Spring
═══ Light Duty		⋎⋏ Rim
≡≡≡≡ Unimproved		⌐ Corral
----- Trail		× Peak
┼┼┼┼ Railroad		Ⓣ Trailhead
■ ■ Buildings		P. Parking
O Water Tank		☁ Water
⚑ Campsite		∼ River
×5270 Elevation Check		∼⸳⸳∼ Drainage

RED RIDGE TRAIL #2

ATTRACTION: A true test of your abilities, visit an old mining area.

REQUIREMENTS: Food, water, sturdy boots, proper maps; car okay to trailhead; 1.5 hours hiking time one way.

LOCATION: Santa Catalina Ranger District - Santa Catalina Mountains, Tucson.

DIFFICULTY: Moderate to Difficult (back up)

ELEVATIONS: 7975' - 5680'

LENGTH: 3.1 miles one way

MAPS REQUIRED: Santa Catalina Mountain Trail and Recreation Map.

PERMIT: No

BIKES: Yes, but not recommended.

EQUESTRIAN: Yes

WATER: Bring your own.

INFORMATION: Be prepared for some harsh descents and ascents on this trail.

FIREARMS: Yes

PETS ON LEASH: Yes

TRAIL INFORMATION

Take the Mt. Lemmon Highway out of Tucson. Just before the ski area, the road splits and the left fork goes to Summerhaven. Take the right fork and, in just under a mile, watch for a sign and a place to pull off.

Trail will climb for only a short time and then will descend Red Ridge via many steep switchbacks. Two-thirds of the way through the hike the trail will head east after leaving the ridge you have been following.

After crossing the east fork of the Cañada Del Oro, the trail terminates at the East Fork Trail.

Try finding evidence of the mining era; it should not be hard to do, mostly upstream.

RED RIDGE TRAIL #2

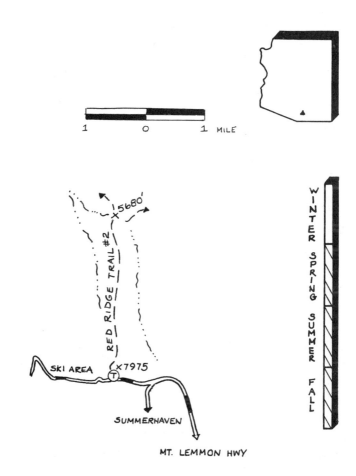

TRUE NORTH

1   O   1   MILE

WINTER SPRING SUMMER FALL

X 5680'

RED RIDGE TRAIL #2

SKI AREA   (T) X 7975

SUMMERHAVEN

MT. LEMMON HWY

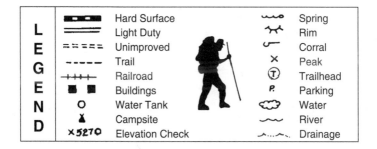

L E G E N D		
Hard Surface		Spring
Light Duty		Rim
Unimproved		Corral
Trail		Peak
Railroad		Trailhead
Buildings		Parking
Water Tank		Water
Campsite		River
×5270 Elevation Check		Drainage

WEST FORK TRAIL #24

ATTRACTION: Another possibility for a hike between Sabino Canyon Visitors Center and the Mt. Lemmon ski area.

REQUIREMENTS: Food, water, sturdy boots, proper maps; car okay to trailhead; 4-5 hours hiking time one way.

LOCATION: Santa Catalina Ranger District - Santa Catalina Mountains.

DIFFICULTY: Moderate

ELEVATIONS: 6100'- 3720'

LENGTH: 6.8 miles one way.

MAPS REQUIRED: Santa Catalina Mountain Trail and Recreation Map.

PERMIT: No   **BIKES:** No   **EQUESTRIAN:** Yes

WATER: Not dependable - bring your own.

INFORMATION: The hike to Mt. Lemmon is long and hard; you might consider descending instead.

FIREARMS: Yes   **PETS ON LEASH:** Yes

TRAIL INFORMATION

Trailhead is at the north end of Sabino Canyon Trail at Sabino Basin. Trail starts to zigzag a bit as you climb gently for 1.5 miles until the next intersection. From here you can take a small side trip to Hutch's Pool, which is a good rest stop, even overnight (a very popular area).

Continuing now past Hutch's Pool, still northwest, the trail crosses West Fork Trail and then drops into and follows it to the Cathedral Rock Trail intersection, via a moderate climb. A left turn here takes you to Cathedral Rock. Continue to the right for 1.8 miles to the Romero Canyon Trail intersection; again, the climb to here is moderate.

Trails included from the Mt. Lemmon ski area are Mt. Lemmon Trail to West Fork Trail to Sabino Canyon Trail, and finally Phone Line Trail to within .5 mile of the Visitors Center. Please refer to *Hiking Arizona II,* which adds some 20 additional trails in this area.

WEST FORK TRAIL #24

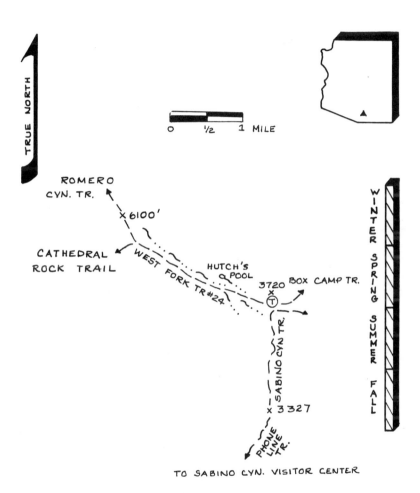

WILDERNESS OF ROCKS
TRAIL #44

ATTRACTION: Very interesting geological area—one of the best in the Catalinas; nice picnicking; nice views.

REQUIREMENTS: Food, water, sturdy boots, proper maps; car okay to Marshall Gulch picnic area; 2 hours hiking time one way.

LOCATION: Santa Catalina Ranger Dist., Santa Catalina Mtns.

DIFFICULTY: Moderate   **ELEVATIONS:** 7280' - 8000'

LENGTH: 4.0 miles one way.

MAPS REQUIRED: Santa Catalina Mountain Trail and Recreation map, basic 15 minute series, U.S. Forest Service.

PERMIT: No   **BIKES:** No

EQUESTRIAN: Mod. to Difficult   **WATER:** Lemmon Creek

INFORMATION: Consult your map for endless possibilities combining this trail with others; hard to follow in some areas.

FIREARMS: Yes   **PETS ON LEASH:** No

TRAIL INFORMATION

By taking Marshall Trail for 1.2 miles along Lemmon Creek from Marshall Gulch picnic area you will arrive at Marshall Saddle and the start of Wilderness of Rocks Trail. A lot of shade is to be enjoyed along this section until you reach the saddle, from which point Aspen Trail goes to the left and Radio Ridge Trail to the right; continue straight. Having your climbing over now, you gradually lose altitude as the trail makes its way through a real "wilderness of rocks". At about the 2.0 mile mark, high above can be seen Lemmon Rock Lookout. The right turn at this intersection is a 2-mile trail that switchbacks to the lookout. This is a tough trail; do not consider it if not in shape.

Trail continues southwest crossing Lemmon Creek two more times and, as the trail gets a little harder to follow, you will find yourself alongside more formations than you can count. Just before trail's end at the intersection of Mt. Lemmon Trail, you will encounter a slight climb to complete your hike. You can build your own hike from here. Consult your map.

WILDERNESS OF ROCKS
TRAIL #44

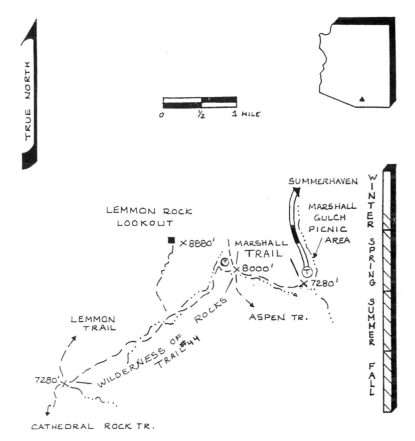

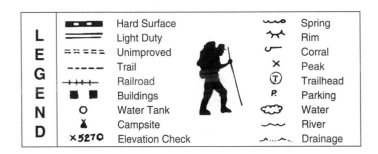

CARR CANYON TRAIL #109

ATTRACTION: Excellent chances for bird and wildlife sightings.

REQUIREMENTS: Food, water, sturdy boots, proper maps; car okay to trailhead; 1.3 hours hiking time one way.

LOCATION: Sierra Vista Ranger District - Huachuca Mountains.

DIFFICULTY: Moderate

ELEVATIONS: 7230' - 6700'

LENGTH: 1.3 miles one way.

MAPS REQUIRED: U.S.G.S. 7.5 min. topographic for Miller Peak.

PERMIT: No, unless returning via Ramsey Preserve. Call the Preserve for information—520-378-2785.

BIKES: No

EQUESTRIAN: No   **WATER:** Bring your own.

INFORMATION: Should you return via Hamburg Trail through the Ramsey Canyon Preserve, call 520-378-2785 for a mandatory permit ahead of time.

FIREARMS: Yes, but not in Ramsey Preserve.

PETS ON LEASH: Yes, but not in Ramsey Preserve.

TRAIL INFORMATION

Follow State Rt. 92 south from the 90/92 junction just east of Sierra Vista. In about 8 miles turn right on Carr Canyon Road (FR #368). Follow FR 368 past the Old Reef Townsite. Trailhead is at the end of FR 368, at the west parking area for the Ramsey Vista camping area. At the western edge of the parking area, there is a double trailhead. The left trail is a spur that, if followed, connects with Carr Peak Trail #107 in a short distance.

Carr Canyon Trail #109 is the right fork. Your descent starts right away as you make your way through an old burn area. Switchbacks are encountered making you think the trail will level off. However, this is not the case as there is a lot of up and down due to several stream crossings. You will cross a fairly flat area just before your final descent to Hamburg Trail #122 and trail's end. Return the same way, or, take Hamburg Trail #122 through the Preserve, you will have to arrange a pick-up or for a shuttle car parked outside the Preserve.

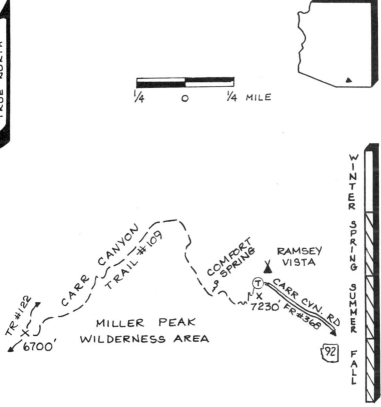

TRUE NORTH

¼ O ¼ MILE

WINTER SPRING SUMMER FALL

CARR CANYON TRAIL #109

COMFORT SPRING

RAMSEY VISTA

T
X
7230'
CARR CYN. RD
FR #368

TR #122
X
6700'

MILLER PEAK
WILDERNESS AREA

92

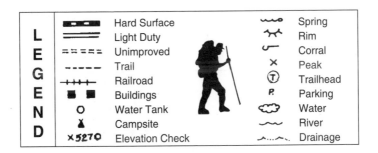

LEGEND

Hard Surface	Spring
Light Duty	Rim
Unimproved	Corral
Trail	× Peak
Railroad	Ⓣ Trailhead
Buildings	P. Parking
O Water Tank	Water
Campsite	River
×5270 Elevation Check	Drainage

CARR PEAK SPUR TRAIL #108

ATTRACTION: Great views from the summit of Carr Peak at 9250'.

REQUIREMENTS: Food, water, sturdy boots, proper maps; car okay to trailhead of Carr Peak Trail #107; 1/2 hour hiking time one way.

LOCATION: Sierra Vista Ranger District - Huachuca Mountains.

DIFFICULTY: Moderate

ELEVATIONS: 8950' - 9250'

LENGTH: .3 mile one way.

MAPS REQUIRED: U.S.G.S. 7.5 min. topographic for Miller Peak.

PERMIT: No

BIKES: No

EQUESTRIAN: Yes

WATER: Bring your own.

INFORMATION: Trailhead is located 1 mile from the end of Carr Peak Trail #107 before it terminates at Crest Trail #103.

FIREARMS: Yes

PETS ON LEASH: Yes

TRAIL INFORMATION

Follow all information on page 78 for the Carr Peak Trail #107 for the start of this trail.

Leaving Carr Peak Trail #107 via a right turn 1 mile before Crest Trail #103, you will climb in kind of a half circle as you ascend to Carr Peak itself. The trail will be rather open for your enjoyment as you reach the treeless summit.

Return the way you came.

CARR PEAK SPUR
TRAIL #108

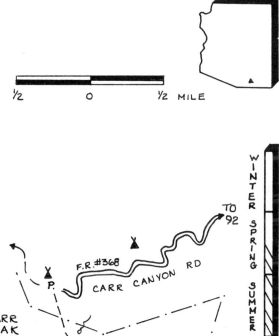

CARR PEAK
TR.#108

CARR
PEAK
9250'

CARR
PEAK

8750'

F.R.#368

CARR CANYON RD

TO 92

MILLER
CANYON
WILDERNESS
AREA

TR.#107

TRUE NORTH

½   O   ½ MILE

WINTER SPRING SUMMER FALL

L E G E N D				
	Hard Surface		Spring	
	Light Duty		Rim	
	Unimproved		Corral	
	Trail	×	Peak	
	Railroad	Ⓣ	Trailhead	
	Buildings	P.	Parking	
o	Water Tank		Water	
	Campsite		River	
×5270	Elevation Check		Drainage	

CARR PEAK TRAIL #107

ATTRACTION: Easiest way to Carr Peak, one of the most popular trails in the Huachucas.

REQUIREMENTS: Food, water, sturdy boots, proper maps; car okay to trailhead; 2.5 hours hiking time one way.

LOCATION: Sierra Vista Ranger District - Huachuca Mountains.

DIFFICULTY: Difficult

ELEVATIONS: 7230' - 8950'

LENGTH: 3.5 miles one way

MAPS REQUIRED: U.S.G.S. 7.5 min. topographic for Miller Peak.

PERMIT: No   **BIKES:** No

EQUESTRIAN: Difficult - not recommended.

WATER: Bring your own.

INFORMATION: You will note old burns and their regeneration on this trail.

FIREARMS: Yes   **PETS ON LEASH:** Yes

TRAIL INFORMATION

Follow State Rt. 92 south from the 90/92 junction just east of Sierra Vista. In about 8 miles will be a right turn onto Carr Canyon Road (FR #368). Follow FR 368 past the Old Reef Townsite. Trailhead is at the end of FR 368 just before Ramsey Vista Campground.

Trail begins from lower parking area out of Ramsey Vista Campground, climbs a ridge and passes the old Sawmill Spring Spur Trail at about .6 mile. Bearing right, you will start switchbacking through different trail conditions due to the trail being subjected to the elements after two old burns. With Carr Peak still above, you will have great views of Miller Peak. The switchbacks continue as does your climb to a trail junction at just under 2.5 miles at Crest Trail #103. However, a right turn at the junction will be Carr Peak Spur Trail #108 to the summit at 9250' (see Carr Peak Spur Trail description).

Many trail options are now possible to build on your hike. Consult your map.

CARR PEAK TRAIL #107

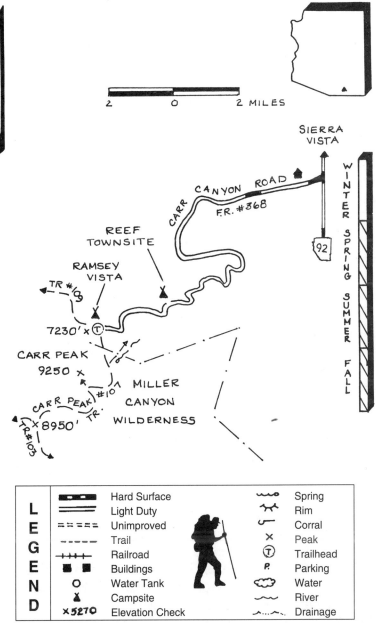

TRUE NORTH

2   0   2 MILES

SIERRA VISTA

CARR CANYON ROAD
F.R. #368

REEF TOWNSITE

RAMSEY VISTA

TR #103

7230' x (T)

CARR PEAK
9250 x

CARR PEAK) #10
TR.

x 8950'

TR #103

MILLER CANYON WILDERNESS

92

WINTER SPRING SUMMER FALL

LEGEND

Hard Surface		Spring
Light Duty		Rim
Unimproved		Corral
Trail		Peak
Railroad		Trailhead (T)
Buildings		Parking P.
Water Tank O		Water
Campsite		River
Elevation Check X5270		Drainage

HAMBURG TRAIL #122

ATTRACTION: A short hike to some very secluded areas.

REQUIREMENTS: Food, water, sturdy boots, proper maps; car okay to trailhead; 2 hours hiking time one way.

LOCATION: Sierra Vista Ranger District - Huachuca Mountains.

DIFFICULTY: Moderate

ELEVATIONS: 5700' - 8075'   **LENGTH:** 4 miles one way.

MAPS REQUIRED: U.S.G.S. 7.5 min. topographic for Miller Peak.

PERMIT: Yes - mandatory if entering through the Preserve.

BIKES: No

EQUESTRIAN: Not through the Preserve, elsewhere okay.

WATER: Yes, but best to bring your own.

INFORMATION: For more information to trailhead access and your mandatory permit, call the Ramsey Canyon Preserve at 520-378-2785.

FIREARMS: No   **PETS ON LEASH:** No

TRAIL INFORMATION

Take Hwy. 92 about 6 miles south of Sierra Vista to the Preserve at the end of Ramsey Canyon Road. Check in at the office with your permit. They will instruct you from there.

Trail begins on an old road through the Preserve passing a very old structure on your right, as well as a cement pond. A very scenic overlook is located at the 1-mile mark. The road ends and the trail heads up the canyon by bearing left. After a few moderate switchbacks you again are on the old road at the overlook.

You will now drop into the canyon, cross the creek and climb the other side where, in about .5 mile, on the right will be the junction of Brown Canyon Trail #115. You will cross the creek several more times, and at just under 2.5 miles at the junction of Carr Canyon Trail. Trail will enter Hamburg Meadow (a nice picnic area) and, after passing through, you will encounter a fork in the trail where Pat Scott Canyon Trail travels west to the Crest Trail. Take the left fork for more creek crossings and switchbacks. Pass an old mine and make a moderate climb to the end of the trail at Bear Saddle. Return the same way.

HAMBURG TRAIL #122

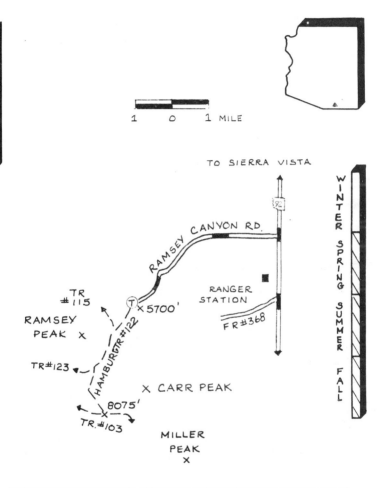

TRUE NORTH

1   0   1 MILE

TO SIERRA VISTA

RAMSEY CANYON RD.

TR #115

RAMSEY PEAK X

TR#123

HAMBURG TR #122

X 5700'

RANGER STATION

FR#368

X CARR PEAK

8075'

TR.#103

MILLER PEAK X

WINTER SPRING SUMMER FALL

LEGEND			
▬▬▬	Hard Surface	ᨆᨆᨆ◦	Spring
═══	Light Duty	ᨆᨆ	Rim
═ ═ ═ ═	Unimproved	ᨆ	Corral
- - - - -	Trail	×	Peak
+++++	Railroad	Ⓣ	Trailhead
■ ■	Buildings	P.	Parking
O	Water Tank	☁	Water
⚑	Campsite	ᨆᨆ	River
×5270	Elevation Check	ᨆ...ᨆ.	Drainage

LAKE SHORE TRAIL #128

ATTRACTION: Camping, hiking, boating, swimming at your own risk, RV's, small store, gas, fishing license.

REQUIREMENTS: Food, water, sturdy boots, proper maps; car okay to trailhead; 2 hours hiking time.

LOCATION: Sierra Vista Ranger District - Coronado National Forest.

DIFFICULTY: Easy

ELEVATIONS: 5375' - 5375'

LENGTH: 5 miles

MAPS REQUIRED: None, trail is very easy to follow.

PERMIT: No

BIKES: No

EQUESTRIAN: No

WATER: Yes, but best to bring your own.

INFORMATION: All rules here are strictly enforced.

FIREARMS: No

PETS ON LEASH: Yes - on leash only.

TRAIL INFORMATION

Take I-10 east out of Tucson and take the State Rt. 83 exit. Follow State Rt. 83 all the way south to Parker Canyon Lake Campground and facilities, and find a proper parking spot. The trail starts anywhere along the lake.

Trail will be easy to follow. Care should be taken on the far side at the spillway. Chances of sighting wildlife are excellent if you stay alert. This trail is a complete loop.

LAKE SHORE TRAIL #128

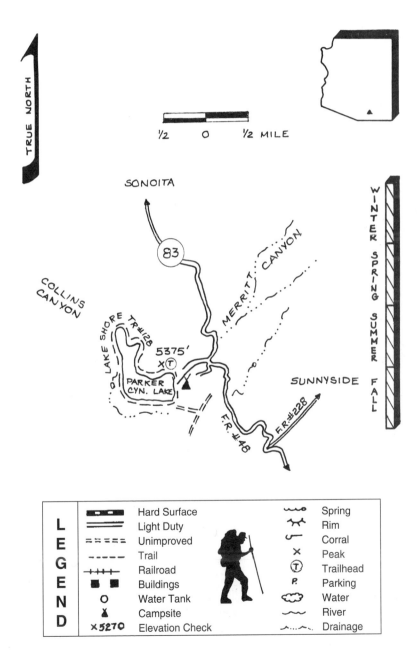

TRUE NORTH

½   0   ½ MILE

SONOITA

COLLINS CANYON

MERRITT CANYON

83

LAKE SHORE TR #128

5375'
X (T)

PARKER CYN. LAKE

SUNNYSIDE

F.R. #48

F.R. #228

WINTER SPRING SUMMER FALL

L E G E N D		Hard Surface		Spring
		Light Duty		Rim
		Unimproved		Corral
		Trail	×	Peak
		Railroad	(T)	Trailhead
		Buildings	P.	Parking
	O	Water Tank		Water
		Campsite		River
	×5270	Elevation Check		Drainage

MILLER CANYON TRAIL #106

ATTRACTION: Good test of your abilities, shortest way to the popular Miller Peak, many fine views.

REQUIREMENTS: Food, water, sturdy boots, proper maps; car okay to trailhead; 3.5 hours hiking time one way.

LOCATION: Sierra Vista Ranger District - Huachuca Mountains.

DIFFICULTY: Moderate to Difficult.

ELEVATIONS: 5775' - 8600'   **LENGTH:** 4 miles one way.

MAPS REQUIRED: U.S.G.S. 7.5 min. topographic for Miller Peak.

PERMIT: No   **BIKES:** No   **EQUESTRIAN:** Difficult

WATER: Yes, but best to bring your own.

INFORMATION: Be prepared for strenuous hiking; your side trip at trail's end to Miller Peak is your reward.

FIREARMS: Yes   **PETS ON LEASH:** Yes

TRAIL INFORMATION

Travel south out of Sierra Vista 9 miles on State Rt. 92 starting from the 90/92 junction. Make a right turn onto the Miller Canyon Road and in about 2.5 miles you will be at the trailhead parking area. The actual trailhead is just across from an old orchard (private property).

After skirting the orchard, the trail joins an old road as you make your way up the canyon. In about .5 mile you will be at the junction with Hunter Canyon Trail #111; continue straight. Just past the junction the road bears to the left and then the trail veers to the right, narrows and gets steeper. At about the 1.5-mile mark, watch for a sign indicating actual hiking trail.

As you now proceed on the foot trail, several switchbacks are encountered. You will come to some old mine workings, a good place to rest before maneuvering more switchbacks that lie ahead. Trail will leave and rejoin the stream many times on this hike. After passing more mining activity and more uphill hiking, you will arrive at the junction of Crest Trail #103 at trail's end. Return the same way, or travel left (south) on Crest Trail #103 for about 1.5 miles to the junction with Miller Peak Trail #105 for its .5-mile ascent to Miller Peak. It's worth it!

MILLER CANYON
TRAIL #106

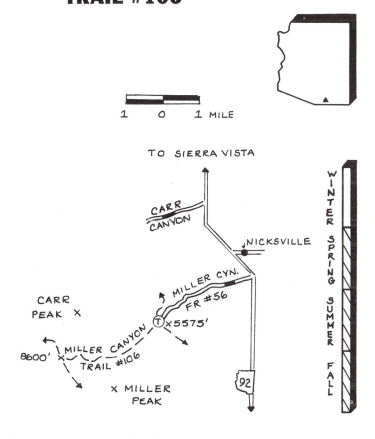

TRUE NORTH

1   0   1 MILE

TO SIERRA VISTA

CARR
CANYON

NICKSVILLE

MILLER CYN.
FR #56

CARR
PEAK X

(T) X5575'

8600' X ——— MILLER CANYON
TRAIL #106

X MILLER
PEAK

92

WINTER SPRING SUMMER FALL

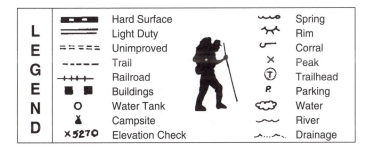

L	Hard Surface		Spring
E	Light Duty		Rim
G	Unimproved		Corral
E	Trail	×	Peak
N	Railroad	(T)	Trailhead
D	Buildings	P.	Parking
	Water Tank		Water
	Campsite		River
X5270	Elevation Check		Drainage

LEGEND

MILLER PEAK TRAIL #105

ATTRACTION: Fantastic views; bring your camera.

REQUIREMENTS: Food, water, sturdy boots, proper maps; car okay to trailhead for Miller Canyon Trail #106; 3/5 hour hiking time one way.

LOCATION: Sierra Vista Ranger District - Huachuca Mountains.

DIFFICULTY: Difficult

ELEVATIONS: 8600' - 9466'

LENGTH: .5 mile one way.

MAPS REQUIRED: U.S.G.S. 7.5 min. topographic for Miller Peak.

PERMIT: No

BIKES: No

EQUESTRIAN: Difficult

WATER: Bring your own

INFORMATION: Trail well marked but has very steep and rocky areas. Be prepared to take your time.

FIREARMS: Yes

PETS ON LEASH: Yes

TRAIL INFORMATION

Follow all directions for Miller Canyon Trail #106 to arrive at the junction of Crest Trail #103 and Miller Peak Trail #105, on the west side of Miller Peak.

You cannot lose your way on this well-beaten path as you switchback your way to this awesome peak. The hike isn't easy but it's worth it.

You have many options to build on your hike. Study your map.

MILLER PEAK TRAIL #105

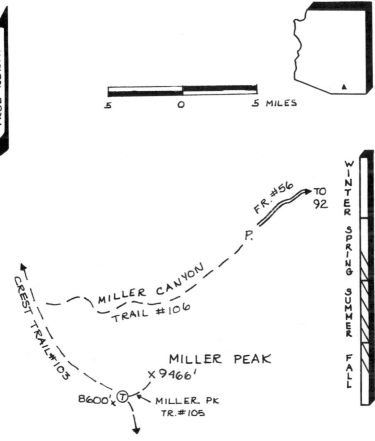

TRUE NORTH

5   0   5 MILES

WINTER SPRING SUMMER FALL

FR. #56 → TO 92

MILLER CANYON
TRAIL #106

CREST TRAIL #103

P.

MILLER PEAK
X 9466'

8600'x (T)   MILLER PK
TR. #105

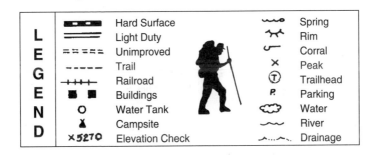

L E G E N D		
▬▬▬ Hard Surface	∿∿○	Spring
──── Light Duty	↔↔	Rim
═ ═ ═ ═ Unimproved	⌐	Corral
- - - - Trail	×	Peak
┼┼┼┼ Railroad	(T)	Trailhead
■ ■ Buildings	P.	Parking
○ Water Tank	⬡	Water
▲ Campsite	∿	River
×5270 Elevation Check	∼...∼.	Drainage

PAT SCOTT CANYON TRAIL #123

ATTRACTION: A short hike to the famous Crest Trail as well as other destinations.

REQUIREMENTS: Food, water, sturdy boots, proper maps; trailhead is located at the end of Hamburg Trail #122; car okay to #122 trailhead; 1.8 hours hiking time one way.

LOCATION: Sierra Vista Ranger District - Huachuca Mountains.

DIFFICULTY: Difficult

ELEVATIONS: 6800' - 8425'   **LENGTH:** 2.1 miles one way

MAPS REQUIRED: U.S.G.S. 7.5 min. topographic for Miller Peak.

PERMIT: Yes - mandatory if entering through the Preserve.

BIKES: No

EQUESTRIAN: Not through the Preserve - elsewhere okay.

WATER: Yes, but best to bring your own.

INFORMATION: For more information to trailhead access and your mandatory permit, call the Ramsey Canyon Preserve at 520-378-2785.

FIREARMS: No   **PETS ON LEASH:** No

TRAIL INFORMATION

Follow all directions to trailhead of Hamburg Trail #122. Follow all directions described for Hamburg Trail itself to a junction where Hamburg Trail bears left and heads up Wisconsin Canyon, and Pat Scott Canyon Trail takes off to the right (west). This is the actual trailhead.

Heading west now on Pat Scott Canyon Trail you can't help but notice the serious flooding that occurred here a few years back, drastically changing the terrain. This was quite a mining area long ago and evidence of a lot of machinery can be seen scattered around by the flood waters.

The climb has been moderate to here and, although the trail gets nicer, you will have several creek crossings and a lot of altitude to gain. Soon you will arrive at the end of the trail at Crest Trail #103. If you have a car at the Preserve, then return the same way. Otherwise you could build on your hike on Crest Trail. Pat Scott Peak Trail #114 is also an option; study your maps.

PAT SCOTT CANYON
TRAIL #123

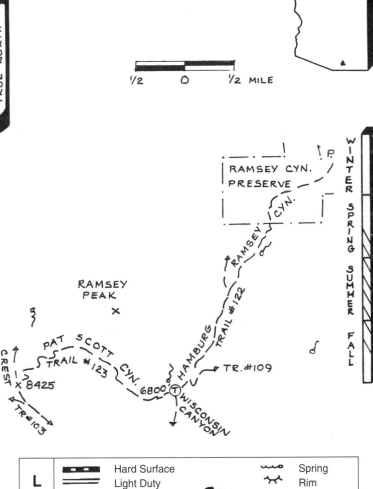

TRUE NORTH

½   0   ½ MILE

WINTER SPRING SUMMER FALL

RAMSEY CYN. PRESERVE

P.

RAMSEY CYN.

RAMSEY PEAK
×

Trail #122

PAT SCOTT

SCOTT CYN.

TRAIL #123

HAMBURG

CREST
× 8425

TR. #103

6800
(T)

TR. #109

WISCONSIN CANYON

LEGEND

▭▬▭	Hard Surface	⌁⌁ Spring
═══	Light Duty	🗙 Rim
═ ═ ═	Unimproved	⌐ Corral
-----	Trail	× Peak
+++++	Railroad	(T) Trailhead
■ ■	Buildings	P. Parking
O	Water Tank	☁ Water
⚑	Campsite	∼ River
×5270	Elevation Check	∼...∼ Drainage

PAT SCOTT PEAK TRAIL #114

ATTRACTION: Nice, short side trip to Pat Scott Peak.

REQUIREMENTS: Food, water, sturdy boots, proper maps; trailhead is located at the junction of Crest and Pat Scott Canyon Trails (see information below); car okay to Hamburg Trail trailhead at the Preserve; 3/4 hour hiking time one way.

LOCATION: Sierra Vista Ranger District - Huachuca Mountains.

DIFFICULTY: Easy to Moderate

ELEVATIONS: 8425' - 8800'

LENGTH: .3 mile one way.

MAPS REQUIRED: U.S.G.S. 7.5 min. topographic for Miller Peak.

PERMIT: Yes - mandatory if entering through the Preserve.

BIKES: No

EQUESTRIAN: Not through the Preserve - elsewhere okay.

WATER: Bring your own.

INFORMATION: If entering through Ramsey Canyon Preserve, you can get information and your mandatory permit by calling 520-378-2785.

FIREARMS: No

PETS ON LEASH: No

TRAIL INFORMATION

Trailhead is located at the junction of Crest Trail #103 and Pat Scott Canyon Trail #123. If you access this trailhead from Pat Scott Canyon Trail, then follow all trail information for it as well as for Hamburg Trail #122.

If you face east, the peak is evident, and a sign was erected to point the way. Do not expect a well-defined trail to the peak, but it is an easy climb.

Return the same way.

PAT SCOTT PEAK
TRAIL #114

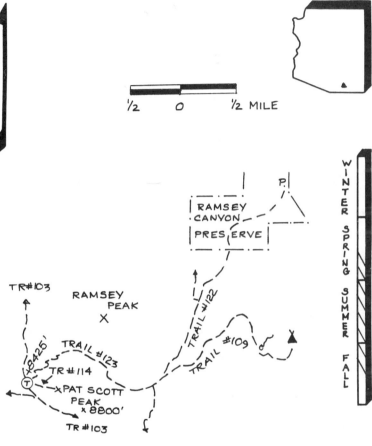

TRUE NORTH

½ 0 ½ MILE

P.

RAMSEY
CANYON
PRESERVE

WINTER SPRING SUMMER FALL

TR#103

RAMSEY
PEAK
X

TRAIL #122

TRAIL #109

X8425'

TRAIL #123

TR #114

TRAIL #109

T

XPAT SCOTT
PEAK
x 8800'

TR #103

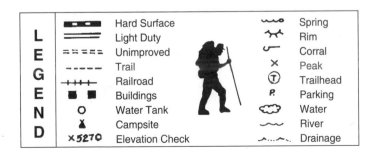

L E G E N D		
▬▬	Hard Surface	
———	Light Duty	
== ====	Unimproved	
- - - - -	Trail	
+++++	Railroad	
■ ■	Buildings	
O	Water Tank	
▲	Campsite	
×5270	Elevation Check	

⌒o	Spring	
⋎⋎	Rim	
⌐	Corral	
×	Peak	
T	Trailhead	
P.	Parking	
⌒⌒	Water	
⌒⌒	River	
⌒...⌒	Drainage	

REEF TOWNSITE LOOP
TRAIL #102

ATTRACTION: Family trail with an historical lesson of its own.

REQUIREMENTS: Food, water, sturdy boots, proper maps; car okay to trailhead; 3/4 hour hiking time.

LOCATION: Sierra Vista Ranger District - Huachuca Mountains.

DIFFICULTY: Moderate

ELEVATIONS: 7000' - 7150'

LENGTH: .7 miles.

MAPS REQUIRED: U.S.G.S. 7.5 min. topographic for Miller Peak.

PERMIT: No

BIKES: No

EQUESTRIAN: No

WATER: Bring your own

INFORMATION: Interpretive Trail.

FIREARMS: No

PETS ON LEASH: Yes

TRAIL INFORMATION

Follow State Rt. 92 from the 90/92 junction just east of Sierra Vista. In about 8 miles, make a right turn onto Carr Canyon Road (Forest Road #368). Follow F.R. 368 to the Reef Townsite camping area and trailhead.

Trail starts from the back parking area. Throughout this short trail, there is a lot of history to be learned by reading the many interpretive signs and explanations about times gone by. It is fascinating to see the old residences and equipment that were abandoned here.

The trail returns to the campground.

REEF TOWNSITE LOOP
TRAIL #102

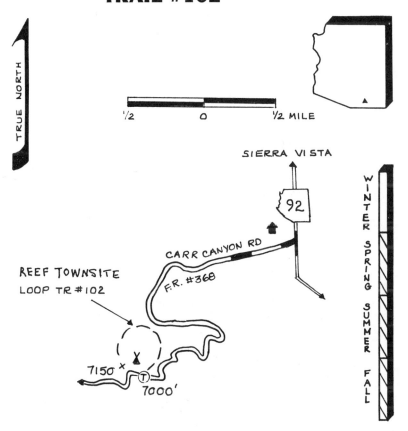

TRUE NORTH

½   0   ½ MILE

SIERRA VISTA

92

CARR CANYON RD

F.R. #368

REEF TOWNSITE
LOOP TR #102

7150 ×

7000'

WINTER SPRING SUMMER FALL

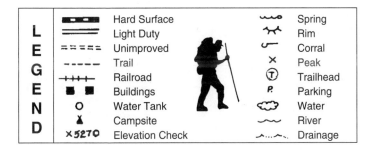

L	▬▬▬	Hard Surface	︶︶○ Spring
E	══	Light Duty	⅀ Rim
G	══ ══	Unimproved	⌐ Corral
	-----	Trail	× Peak
E	+++++	Railroad	Ⓣ Trailhead
N	▪ ▪	Buildings	P. Parking
D	O	Water Tank	� Water
	▲	Campsite	∿ River
	×5270	Elevation Check	⌒‥⌒. Drainage

Hiking the Wilderness of Rocks Trail.
(Photo by John Villinski)

Granite boulder on the Wilderness of Rocks Trail.
(Photo by John Villinski)

HIKING SOUTHERN ARIZONA RANGER DISTRICTS

Contact the following for more information:

Douglas Ranger District
R.R. 1, Box 228-R
Douglas, AZ 85607 520-364-3468
- Jhus-Horse Saddle Trail #252
- Morman Canyon Trail #352
- Morman Ridge Trail #269
- Morse Canyon Trail #43
- Pinery-Horsefall Trail #336
- Pole Bridge Trail #264
- Rattlesnake Trail #275
- Saulsbury Trail #263
- Shaw Peak Trail #251
- South Fork Trail #243

Nogales Ranger District
2251 N. Grand Avenue
Nogales, AZ 85621 520-281-2296
- Armour Spring Trail #71
- Atascosa Trail #100
- Bog Springs Trail #156
- Crest Trail #144
- Dutch John Trail #91
- Florida Canyon Trail #145
- Kent Spring Trail #157
- Old Baldy Trail #372
- Super Trail #134
- Sycamore Trail #40

Santa Catalina Ranger District
5700 N. Sabino Canyon Road
Tucson, AZ 85715 520-749-8700
- Bear Canyon Trail #29
- Butterfly Trail #16
- Crystal Spring Trail #17
- Italian Spring Trail #95

(Continued on next page)

- Marshall Gulch Trail #3
- Meadow Trail #5A
- Mount Lemmon Trail #5
- Red Ridge Trail #2
- West Fork Trail #24
- Wilderness of Rocks Trail #44

Sierra Vista Ranger District
5990 S. Highway 92
Hereford, AZ 85615 520-378-0311
- Carr Canyon Trail #109
- Carr Peak Spur Trail #108
- Carr Peak Trail #107
- Hamburg Trail #122
- Lakeshore Trail #128
- Miller Canyon Trail #106
- Miller Peak Trail #105
- Pat Scott Canyon Trail #123
- Pat Scott Peak Trail #114
- Reef Town Site Loop Trail #102

Weather—Great, but Changeable

The saying goes, if you don't like the weather in Arizona, then just wait a few minutes.

This is a fine example of how fast a change can occur and, depending on how far you are out on the trail, and if unprepared, can be the start of your demise.

Arizona's wide array of extremes from the hot arid desert to the cool (if not freezing) lofty peaks carries with it the perfect ingredients for you to be concerned—concerned enough to never travel unprepared!

July and August are the most unpredictable months. Fast growing storms in the mountains and on the desert can cause flash floods and severe drops in temperature.

Always check weather conditions and forecasts before you travel the trails. Again I will stress that you go prepared in every way you can, and be informed!

Trail Etiquette

Let's face it, if you meet someone on the trail, they are there to have a good time and get away from it all, the same as you. If everyone exercises courtesy and cooperation, then everyone has a better time.

Trail etiquette also means having respect for the trail itself. Do not cut switchbacks on a trail. Switchbacks are built to make the trail easier, cutting them only makes your hike harder and causes erosion that damages the trail.

Downhill hikers must always yield to hikers coming uphill, and do it in such a way as to not break their stride or concentration.

If you are hiking faster than the party ahead of you, slow down and wait for them to allow you to pass at an ideal location; thank them.

If you stop for a rest, do so well off the trail, in order to give others a clear path to travel.

Do not hike or ride bikes on wet trails as this activity can cause permanent damage to the trails.

All trail users must yield to all trail stock. These animals can be excitable, and if you are not calm and quiet a rider (or even you) could be badly injured.

If you are allowed a pet on the trail, keep it on a leash. Be careful that you are clear of other hikers so the leash will not trip them.

Loud noises or yelling without reason is distracting to all. Allow others to enjoy the wilderness atmosphere without unnecessary noises.

If we all work together, we can make the great outdoors a pleasant place for everyone, now, as well as in the future.

CONTENTS OF YOUR DAY PACK

Listed below are the items I feel comfortable with. Feel free to add or subtract to suit your needs. Keep in mind that you may be planning a day hike that could turninto an overnite stay for a variety of reasons. Go prepared!

1. Small flashlight, bulbs and batteries
2. Candies that will not melt or spoil
3. Whistle (a police whistle is ideal)
4. Good compass
5. Toilet paper
6. Complete first aid kit
7. Salt tablets
8. Strong sunscreen
9. Any medicines or prescriptions you require
10. Pocket knife
11. Pencil and paper
12. Lighter and waterproof matches
13. Moleskin
14. Lip salve
15. Bug spray for body
16. One day extra food that will not spoil
17. Leakproof canteen and extra water
18. Enough clothing for overnight stay if necessary
19. Plastic bag for litter
20. Raingear
21. Hat
22. Gloves or mittens
23. Sunglasses
24. Maps and Permits
25. Camera and film
26. Identification

I will stress that your maps are valuable only if you study them very carefully before you leave. Be sure you have chosen a hike that is correct for your capabilities.

Let your friends or family know where you are going, when you expect to return and then stick to that plan!

CONTENTS OF YOUR BACKPACK

Backpacks are used primarily for multiple day outings. Be sure your pack is large enough and fits perfectly. Add the following items to your Day Pack List:

1. Sleeping bag and bed roll.
2. Tent
3. Camping stove and extra fuel.

WHAT TO WEAR FOR MOUNTAIN HIKING

In the "Desert Survival" chapter in this book are hints on proper dress for the desert, but mountain dress has a different application. Mountain dress has its variables for lower rolling hills or higher rugged peaks.

LOWER ROLLING HILLS

In these gentle areas, one can use with great comfort the lightweight hiking boots that are popular today. It's not too likely you will need extreme support for lower elevations. Most of these hikes are one-day outings or shorter, so a heavy backpack need not be carried making heavy footgear unnecessary.

Hiking shorts or denim pants work well here, as it is not likely to be cold. I prefer long sleeves and a hat to prevent sunburn. A day pack works well on shorter hikes of this nature. Sweat shirt and raingear are a must.

HIGHER RUGGED PEAKS

In this kind of hiking one must have a very rugged hiking boot, not only for traction, but also for the ever-present need for good support. Some hikers even buy their boots a half size too large, making room for two pair of socks for more comfort. If you do not buy waterproof boots, then at least spray them with one of the products available to help them repel water.

Denim jeans wear well but do not provide much warmth in extreme cold. If you do wear them hiking, then consider carrying a warmer pair of pants and longjohns in case conditions turn colder. T-shirts are most comfortable under your outer shirts. Notice I said "shirts." I find wearing a couple of shirts instead of one heavy one makes it easier to adjust one's temperature by wearing only what is needed instead of too much or too little.

A warm hat, scarf and mittens and heavy jacket should also be carried on these hikes.

WHAT TO DO WHEN YOU ARE LOST OR INJURED

You might think food, water, proper clothing, or even being attacked by wild animals are the most important concerns if you are lost in the wilderness.

However, all of the above are secondary or even immaterial if you do not exercise self-control. If you allow yourself to panic, then indeed you are lost and will probably only be found by accident. Understandably, this situation can instill fear, but do not give in to it!

Don't wander about. Sit down, relax and very carefully try to run through your mind the events that led up to your becoming lost.

If you fail to figure out what went wrong but you still have plenty of daylight left, travel slowly in the direction you feel is correct. Make sure that if you had been climbing that you now travel only downhill.

If you come to a stream, do not leave it unless, of course, you have found your trail. A stream can almost always supply you with water and food and usually leads to civilization as well.

Keep a very close eye on the daylight you have left. If your daylight will soon be gone, you should immediately find a place to camp overnight. Gather whatever rocks or stones are available, place them in a circle to make a place for a safe fire and gather a supply of wood. You should have a fire burning by the time it becomes dark, eaten whatever food you have allowed for your meal and know where everything in your camp is located.

If you cannot build a fire and do not have a blanket or bedroll, then cover yourself with sticks and leaves to escape the cold and wind; it works!

If you are injured and cannot travel, then a signal fire is your best bet. A very smoky fire by day and a bright fire at night has the best chance of bringing results. You can see how important the contents of your backpack or day pack can become.

Again, stay calm! Things can take a brighter outlook in the morning. It has been proven over and over that a clear head can get you out of almost any situation.

COPING WITH HYPOTHERMIA

Hypothermia is a progressive physical and mental collapse that accompanies the cooling of the inner core of the body. It is the primary killer of outdoor recreationists. Symptoms include a feeling of being extremely cold, uncontrollable shivering and incoherent speech.

Getting wet in rain, sleet, snow or heavy fog or even perspiring, along with a moderately cool wind, can start the process at any time or altitude.

More than half your body's heat is lost from your head and neck being exposed. Obviously, then, a good winter hat with ear tabs, along with a scarf, will do a lot to slow down your major heat loss.

Other susceptible areas are your hands and feet. Mittens will keep you hands warmer than gloves, as the air around your hands will act as insulation. Waterproof boots will take care of your feet.

Some rain gear only drapes your upper body and allows your lower pant legs and boots to get soaking wet. A two-piece coat and pants set is better protection.

If you think that you or someone in your party may be suffering from hypothermia, get the person into dry clothes and get a fire started. It is most important to eat. Food will cause your body to develop heat from the digestion process. Administering warm drinks is also extremely beneficial.

If possible, get the person into a prewarmed sleeping bag heated either at your fire or by having someone lie down in it. Build an insulation barrier with leaves, etc., on which to lay the sleeping bag and to keep it out of the wind.

If the patient is going into severe hypothermia, strip him and yourself of clothing and get into the sleeping bag together. There is no faster way to convey body heat.

When planning a hike, think hypothermia. When shopping for hiking gear, when planning your backpack or day pack, think hypothermia!

SAFETY RULES
FOR SURVIVAL IN THE DESERT

(Courtesy Maricopa County Civil Defense and Emergency Services)

1. Never go into the desert without first informing someone as to your destination, your route and when you will return. STICK TO YOUR PLAN.

2. Carry at least one gallon of water per person per day of your trip. Plastic jugs are handy and portable.

3. Be sure your vehicle is in good condition.

4. KEEP AN EYE ON THE SKY. Flash floods may occur any time "thunder-heads" are in sight, even though it may not rain where you are.

5. If your vehicle breaks down, stay near it. Your emergency supplies are here. Raise your hood and trunk lid to denote "Help Needed"

6. If you are POSITIVE of the route to help, and must leave your vehicle, leave a note for rescuers as to when you left and the direction you are taking.

7. If you have water — DRINK IT. Do not ration it.

8. If water is limited — KEEP YOUR MOUTH SHUT. Do not talk, do not eat, do not smoke, do not drink alcohol, do not take salt.

9. Do not sit or lie DIRECTLY on the ground. It may be 30 degrees or more hotter than the air.

10. A roadway is a sign of civilization. IF YOU FIND A ROAD, STAY ON IT.

The Desert Southwest is characterized by brilliant sunshine, a wide tempera-ture range, sparse vegetation, a scarcity of water, a high rate of evaporation and low annual rainfall.

Travel in the desert can be an interesting and enjoyable experience or it can be a fatal or near fatal nightmare. The contents of this manual can give only a few of the details necessary for full enjoyment of our desert out-of-doors.

If you think you are lost, do not panic. Sit down for a while, survey the area and take stock of the situation. Try to remember how long it has been since you knew where you were. Decide on a course of action. It may be best to stay right where you are and let your companions or rescuers look for you. This is especially true if there is water and fuel nearby or if there is some means of shelter. Once you decide to remain, make a fire — a smoky one for daytime and a bright one for the night. Other signals may be used, but fire is by far the best.

REMEMBER, MOVE WITH A PURPOSE, NEVER START OUT AND WANDER AIMLESSLY.

Walking: There are special rules and techniques for walking in the desert. By walking slowly and resting about 10 minutes per hour a man in good physical condition can cover about 12-18 miles per day — less after he becomes fatigued or lacks sufficient water or food. On the hot desert it is best to travel early morning or late evening, spending mid-day in whatever shade may be available. In walking, pick the easiest and safest way. Go around obstacles, not over them. Instead of going up or down steep slopes, zigzag to prevent undue exertion. Go around gullies and canyons instead of through them. When walking with companions, adjust the rate to the slowest man. Keep together but allow about 10 feet between members.

At rest stops, if you can sit down in the shade and prop your feet up, remove your shoes and change socks, or straighten out the ones you are wearing. If the ground is too hot to sit on, no shade is available, and you cannot raise your feet, do not remove your shoes as you may not be able to get them back onto swollen feet.

Automobile Driving: Cross country driving or driving on little used roads is hazardous, but can be done successfully if a few simple rules are followed. Move slowly. Do not attempt to negotiate washes without first checking the footing and the clearances. High centers may rupture the oil pan. Overhang may cause the driving wheels to become suspended above the ground. Do not spin wheels in an attempt to gain motion, but apply power very slowly to prevent wheel spin and subsequent digging in. When driving in sand, traction can be increased by partially deflating tires. Start, stop and turn gradually, as sudden motions cause wheels to dig in. There are certain tool and equipment requirements if you intend to drive off the main roads: a shovel, a pick-mattock, a tow chain or cable, at least 50 feet of strong tow rope, tire pump, axe, water cans, gas cans, and of course, your regular spare parts and auto tools.

Clothing: For the desert, light-weight and light colored clothing which covers the whole body is best. Long trousers and long sleeves protect from the sun, help to prevent dehydration and protect against insects, abrasions and lacerations by rocks and brush. Headgear should provide all-around shade as well as eye shade.

Survival Kit: Items that should be carried on the individual are: a sharp knife, a signal mirror, a map of the area, thirty or more feet of nylon string, canteen, matches, a snake bite kit, a firearm and ammunition, and other items that may be useful. Consider carrying your gear in a small rucksack or pack over your shoulders. Weight carried in this manner is less tiring than if carried in pockets or hung on the belt. The pack can be used to sit upon. It also affords a safer method of carrying items, such as the belt knife, hatchet, etc., which may lend to the chances of injury in case of a fall.

Health Hazards: Thought must be given to protecting your health and well-being, and the prevention of fatigue and injury: first, because medical assistance will be some distance away; second, because conditions are usually different and distinct from your everyday living. The desert is a usually healthy environment due to dryness, the lack of human and animal wastes, and the sterilizing effect of the hot sun. Therefore, your immediate bodily needs will be your first consideration.

If you are walking or active, rest 10 minutes each hour. Drink plenty of water, especially early in the morning while the temperature is still low.

While in the desert, wear sun glasses to protect your eyes from glare. Even though the glare does not seem to bother you, it will impair your distant vision and will retard your adaptation to night conditions. If you have no glasses make an eyeshade by slitting a piece of paper, cardboard or cloth. Applying charcoal or soot around the eyes is also beneficial.

In a survival situation everything that you do, each motion that you make, and each step you take must be preceded by the thought: am I safe in doing this?

Keep your clothing on, including shirt and hat. Clothing helps ration your sweat by slowing the evaporation rate and prolonging the cooling effect. It also keeps out the hot desert air and reflects the heat of the sun.

Rationing water at high temperatures is actually inviting disaster because small amounts will not prevent dehydration. Loss of efficiency and collapse always follows dehydration. It is the water in your body that maintains your life, not the water in your canteen.

Keep the mouth shut and breathe through the nose to reduce water loss and drying of mucous membranes. Avoid conversation for the same reason. If possible, cover lips with grease or oil. Alcohol in any form is to be avoided as it will accelerate dehydration. Consider alcohol as food and not as water since additional water is required to assimilate the alcohol. For the same reason, food intake should be kept to a minimum if sufficient water is not available.

Carrying Water: When planning to travel, give your water supply extra thought. Do not carry water in glass containers as these may break. Metal insulated containers are good, but heavy. Carry some water in gallon or half-gallon plastic containers similar to those containing bleach. They are unbreakable, light-weight and carrying several will assure a water supply if one is damaged.

Finding Water in the Desert: If you are near water it is best to remain there and prepare signals for your rescuers. If no water is immediately available look for it, following these leads:

Watch for desert trails — following them may lead to water or civilization, particularly if several such trails join and point toward a specific location.

Flocks of birds will circle over water holes. Listen for their chirping in the morning and evening, and you may be able to locate their watering spot. Quail move toward water in the late afternoon and away in the morning. Doves flock toward watering spots morning and evening. Also look for indications of animals as they tend to feed near water.

Look for plants which grow only where there is water: cottonwoods, sycamores, willows, hackberry, saltcedar, cattails and arrow weed. You may have to dig to find this water. Also keep on the lookout for windmills and water tanks built by ranchers. If cactus fruits are ripe, eat a lot of them to help prevent dehydration.

Methods of Purifying Water: Dirty water should be filtered through several layers of cloth or allowed to settle. This does not purify the water even though it may look clean. Purification to kill germs must be done by one of the following methods:

1. Water purification tablets are the easiest to use. Get them from the drug store and follow the directions on the label. Let stand for thirty minutes.

2. Tincture of Iodine: add three drops per quart of clear water, double for cloudy water. Let stand for thirty minutes.

3. Boiling for 3 to 5 minutes will purify most water.

Food: You must have water to survive, but you can go without food for a few days without harmful effects. In fact, if water is not available, do not eat, as food will only increase your need for water. The important thing about locating food in a survival situation is to know what foods are available in the particular invironment and how to obtain them. Hawks soaring overhead may mean water is nearby. Game will be found around water holes and areas that have heavy brush growth.

Edible Wildlife: Almost every animal, reptile and insect is edible. Learn how to prepare the various things that would be available to you in a survival situation. Avoid any small mammal which appears to be sick. Some animals have scent glands which must be removed before cooking. Do not allow the animal hair to come in contact with the flesh as it will give the meat a disagreeable taste.

1. Jack Rabbit: A hare, with long ears and legs, sandy color. Grubs are often found in the hide or flesh but these do not affect the food value.

2. Cottontail Rabbit: Small, pale gray with white tail. Active in the early morning and late evening.

3. Javelina: Dark gray-black, weighing 30-50 pounds with strong tusks. Has scent glands on the back, over the hind legs. May be dangerous if cornered or wounded.

4. Mourning Dove: Year-round resident, usually found near habitation and water.

5. Gambel's Quail, Scaled Quail, Mearn's Quail: The Gambel's is of primary importance in desert and semi-arid areas.

6. Snakes: Most snakes are edible. Rattlesnake is especially good.

7. Desert Tortoise.

Edible Plants: The main desert edibles are the fruits of the cacti and legumes. All cactus fruits are safe to eat. In the summer the fleshy and thin-walled ripe fruits can be singed over a fire to remove spines. Then they can be peeled and eaten. Old cactus fruits contain seeds which can be pounded between two stones into a powder and eaten, or mixed with water into a gruel. New, young pads of the prickly pear can be singed, peeled and boiled.

The legumes are the bean bearing plants. The main ones are the mesquite, the palo verde, the ironwood and the catclaw. All are small trees with fern-like leaves. All have bean pods which when green and tender can be boiled and eaten. Dry, mature beans, like cactus seeds, are too hard to chew and must be cooked.

In a survival situation, where the use of strange plants for food is indicated, follow these rules: Avoid plants with milky sap. Avoid all red beans. If possible, boil plants which are questionable. Test a cooked plant by holding a small quantity in the mouth for a few moments. If the taste is disagreeable, do not eat it.

Fires and Cooking: Clear an area about 15 feet across, dig a pit or arrange rocks to contain the fire. Make a starting fire of dry grass, small twigs, shavings, under-bark of cottonwoods, etc. Place larger twigs — about pencil size — on top. Have heavier material ready to add, using the small pieces first. Place them on the fire in a "tepee" fashion to prevent smothering your starting fire and aid in the formation of an up-draft. After the fire is burning well, continue to use the tepee method for boiling but criss-cross fuel for forming coals for frying or broiling.

Start your fire with a lighter, matches, or a hand lens. Remember, do not use up your water-proofed matches unless your return from the field is a guaranteed fact. Here are some hints for expeditious fire building.

Drying matches: Damp wooden matches can be dried by stroking 20 to 30 times through the dry hair at the side of the head. Be careful not to knock off the chemical head of very wet matches at the start of the procedure.

Tinder: (All of these must be dry.) Under-bark of the cottonwood, cedar bark, dead goldenrod tops, cattail floss, charred cloth, bird nests, mouse nests, or any readily flammable material shredded into fine fibers.

Fuzz-stick: Cut slivers into soft wood sticks and arrange them tepee fashion with the separated ends downward.

Quick, hot fires: Cottonwood, cactus skeletons, creosote-bush, aspen, tamarisk, cedar, pine, and spruce.

Long-lasting fires: Mesquite, ironwood, black jack, sage, and oak.

REMEMBER, YOU WANT FLAME FOR HEAT, EMBERS FOR COOKING, AND FOR SIGNALS YOU NEED SMOKE IN THE DAYTIME AND BRIGHT FIRES AT NIGHT. BE SURE TO EXTINGUISH YOUR FIRE BEFORE LEAVING IT!

Poisonous Creatures: There is probably more said and less truth about poisonous creatures than any other subject. These animals and insects are for the most part shy, or due to their nature, not often seen. Learn the facts about these creatures and you will see that they are not to be feared but only respected.

Snakes: There are many types of snakes in the southwest but only rattlesnakes and coral snakes are poisonous. Snakes hibernate during the colder months, but will start appearing with the warming trend, sometimes in early February. During the spring and fall months they may be found out in the daytime, but during the summer months they will generally be found out during the night, due to the fact that they cannot stand excessive heat.

Rattlesnakes: These are easily identified by the sandy color, the broad arrow-shaped head, blunt tipped-up nose, and rattles on the tail. Look for them mostly where food, water, and protection is available — around abandoned structures, irrigation ditches, water holes, brush and rock piles. They do not always give warning by rattling, nor do they always strike if one is close. If travelling in areas where rattlers are, wear protective footgear and watch where you put your hands and feet.

Arizona Coral Snake: A small snake, rarely over 20 inches long with small blunt, black head and tapering tail. Wide red and black bands are separated by narrower yellow bands and all completely encircle the body. They are noctunal and live under objects, in burrows, and are shy and timid. Corals bite and chew rather than strike, but due to the very small mouth they are unable to bite any but the smallest extremities.

Treatment of Poisonous Snakebite: If bitten, try to capture the snake as identification will aid in specific medical treatment.

1. KEEP THE VICTIM QUIET AND SEEK MEDICAL HELP.

2. If the "cut and suck" method is deemed necessary, follow the instructions with the snake bite kit. In any event, step 1 above, is very important.

Poisonous Insects and Spiders: The potentially lethal species in this area are the scorpion and the black widow spider.

Prevention and Treatment: In places where venomous species are expected, inspect all clothing and bedding before use, especially items that have been on or near the ground. If bitten (stung), get to a doctor, especially if the victim is a child, is elderly, has a bad heart, or has been bitten several times or on the main part of the body.

Index

About the Author

With a degree in Wildlife/Forestry Conservation, it is not surprising that Don Kiefer spends as much time as possible outdoors. Don's books share his experiences and practical knowledge of hiking Arizona.

He has done volunteer work with the National Park Service, recording over 500 hours in the Rincon Wilderness looking for those needing help. The National Forest Service, Pima County Parklands Foundation and Arizona State Parks have also benefitted from Don's services. He has logged over 1,000 hiking miles as a member of the Prevention Walking Society, and an overall total of 4,000 miles of hiking throughout Arizona.

Having learned to fly, Don is especially proud to be an honorary member of the 161st Air Refueling Group at Sky Harbor Airport.

Don began sharing his outdoor world when he started writing for the *Mesa Tribune*. He has now completed five hiking books on Arizona. At the same time, he has been working hard on a hiking library of his own which already consists of 42 volumes, and when complete, will cover every trail in the state.

Don has been cited twice by the National Forest Service and as many times by the National Park Service. He has been honored by B. Dalton Booksellers, as well as Senator John McCain, for his willingness to share his world and his time with everyone. On the wall of Don's office is the Presidential Sports Award received from President George Bush in 1991.

Don is currently working on new hiking books and a book about "haunted" Arizona.

About the Artist

Robyn Wasserman graduated with degrees in Forest Recreation and Natural Resource Management. She has resided in Arizona for 14 years and worked as a park naturalist, hiking guide, fire dispatcher, nursery caretaker and tour guide.

Currently living in Southern Arizona, Robyn is employed as a ranger with Arizona State Parks. When not working, she enjoys hiking, reading, gardening, photography, nature crafts and spending time with her friends.

More Hiking Books by Don R. Kiefer
Discover the Beauty of Outdoor Arizona!

Author Don Kiefer brings you over 200 hikes throughout the great state of Arizona. Each hike has a detailed map, hiking time, distance, difficulty, elevation, attractions, etc. Perfect for novice or experienced hikers. Each book advises what to wear, what to take, safety tips, what to do when lost, trail etiquette and more!

HIKING ARIZONA

50 hiking trails from the San Francisco Peaks to the Mexican border. Hike Mt. Humphreys (highest mountain in Arizona), enjoy the South Mountain Trails of Phoenix and explore the unique beauty of the Santa Catalina, Rincon and Tucson mountains of southern Arizona.

5 1/2 x 8 1/2— 160 pages . . . $6.95

HIKING ARIZONA II

50 hiking trails take you throughout the great state of Arizona! Hike the Inner Basin and Abinau Trails of the San Francisco Peaks. Enjoy the Aravaipa Canyon Wilderness Area of central Arizona and then on to the challenging Sendero Esperanza Trail in the Saguaro National Monument in the Tucson Mountains.

5 1/2 x 8 1/2— 160 pages . . . $6.95

HIKING CENTRAL ARIZONA

40 great trails from the deserts of Arizona to the beautiful Mogollon Rim forests. Hike the Seven Springs Recreational Area trails of Cave Creek and follow the Raspberry Trail in the Blue Ridge Primite Area near Hannagan Meadow. Unmatched views of deserts, valleys, mountain peaks and more await you!

5 1/2 x 8 1/2— 120 pages . . . $5.95

HIKING NORTHERN ARIZONA

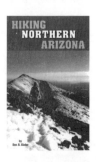

40 trails featuring the beauty of northern Arizona. From the Grand Canyon's beautiful Nankoweap Trail south to the Red Rocks of Sedona and east to the Mogollon Rim and the Escudilla and Steeple Mesa Trails . . . you will hike some of the most beautiful areas that can be found in the Southwest!

5 1/2 x 8 1/2— 112 pages . . . $5.95

SNAKES and other REPTILES
of the SOUTHWEST

This book is a must for hikers, hunters, campers and all outdoor enthusiasts! More than 80 photographs and illustrations in the text and full color plate insert, this book is the definitive, easy-to-use guide to Southwestern reptiles! By Erik Stoops and Annette Wright.

6 x 9 — 128 Pages . . . $9.95

SCORPIONS and VENOMOUS INSECTS of the SOUTHWEST

A user-friendly guide to the wide variety of scorpions and other venomous creatures of the Southwest. Scorpions, spiders, ticks and mites, centipedes, millipedes, bees and more are shown in detailed illustrations and full color photos. By Erik Stoops and Jeffrey Martin.

5 1/2 x 8 1/2 — 112 Pages . . . $9.95

EXPLORE ARIZONA!

Where to find old coins, bottles, fossil beds, arrowheads, petroglyphs, waterfalls, ice caves, cliff dwellings. Detailed maps to 59 Arizona wonders! By Rick Harris.

5 1/2 x 8 1/2— 128 pages . . . $6.95

DISCOVER ARIZONA!

Enjoy the thrill of discovery! Prehistoric ruins, historic battlegrounds, fossil beds, arrowheads, rock crystals and semi-precious stones! By Rick Harris.

5 1/2 x 8 1/2 — 112 Pages . . . $6.95

HORSE TRAILS IN ARIZONA

Complete guide to over 100 of Arizona's most beautiful equestrian trails, from the desert to the high country. Maps, directions to trailheads, water availability and more to ensure an unmatched experience for all who love hoseback riding. Lodging and "hitchin' post" restaurant information, too! By Jan Hancock.

5 1/2 x 8 1/2 — 160 Pages . . . $9.95

ORDER BLANK

GOLDEN WEST PUBLISHERS

☼ 4113 N. Longview Ave. • Phoenix, AZ 85014

602-265-4392 • **1-800-658-5830** • FAX 602-279-6901

Qty	Title	Price	Amount
	Arizona Museums	9.95	
	Arizona—Off the Beaten Path	6.95	
	Arizona Outdoor Guide	6.95	
	Cactus Country	6.95	
	Discover Arizona!	6.95	
	Explore Arizona!	6.95	
	Fishing Arizona	7.95	
	Ghost Towns in Arizona	6.95	
	Hiking Arizona	6.95	
	Hiking Arizona II	6.95	
	Hiking Central Arizona	5.95	
	Hiking Northern Arizona	5.95	
	Hiking Southern Arizona	5.95	
	Horse Trails in Arizona	9.95	
	Motorcycle Arizona!	9.95	
	Prehistoric Arizona	5.00	
	Scorpions & Venomous Insects of the SW	9.95	
	Snakes and other Reptiles of the SW	9.95	
	Sedona Cook Book	7.95	
	Verde River Recreation Guide	6.95	

Add $2.00 to total order for shipping & handling **$2.00**

☐ My Check or Money Order Enclosed. . . . . $ _____

☐ MasterCard   ☐ VISA

Acct. No. _____ Exp. Date _____

Signature _____

Name _____ Telephone _____

Address _____

City/State/Zip _____

Call for FREE catalog

11/95   MasterCard and VISA Orders Accepted ($20 Minimum)

Hiking S.

This order blank may be photo-copied.